CAMBRIDGE LIBRARY COLLECTION

Books of enduring scholarly value

Printing and Publishing History

The interface between authors and their readers is a fascinating subject in its own right, revealing a great deal about social attitudes, technological progress, aesthetic values, fashionable interests, political positions, economic constraints, and individual personalities. This part of the Cambridge Library Collection reissues classic studies in the area of printing and publishing history that shed light on developments in typography and book design, printing and binding, the rise and fall of publishing houses and periodicals, and the roles of authors and illustrators. It documents the ebb and flow of the book trade supplying a wide range of customers with products from almanacs to novels, bibles to erotica, and poetry to statistics.

The Origin of Printing

This work, first published in 1774, consists of a reissue of the *Dissertation on the Origin of Printing in England* by Conyers Middleton (1683–1750), first published in 1735, together with an abridgement of an account of the origin of printing by the Dutch lawyer Gerard Meerman (1722–71). It was compiled by the scholar and publisher William Bowyer (1699–1777) and his apprentice and later business partner John Nichols (1745–1826), several of whose works are also published in this series. Both essays debate the origins of printing, disputing the traditional account that Gutenberg introduced it to Europe and Caxton to England. Appendices describe the progress of printing in Greek and Hebrew, and the first printed polyglot Bibles. The names and achievements of Gutenberg's contemporaries in Germany and the Low Countries are given their due in this interesting overview of the earliest period of printing in the West.

Cambridge University Press has long been a pioneer in the reissuing of out-of-print titles from its own backlist, producing digital reprints of books that are still sought after by scholars and students but could not be reprinted economically using traditional technology. The Cambridge Library Collection extends this activity to a wider range of books which are still of importance to researchers and professionals, either for the source material they contain, or as landmarks in the history of their academic discipline.

Drawing from the world-renowned collections in the Cambridge University Library and other partner libraries, and guided by the advice of experts in each subject area, Cambridge University Press is using state-of-the-art scanning machines in its own Printing House to capture the content of each book selected for inclusion. The files are processed to give a consistently clear, crisp image, and the books finished to the high quality standard for which the Press is recognised around the world. The latest print-on-demand technology ensures that the books will remain available indefinitely, and that orders for single or multiple copies can quickly be supplied.

The Cambridge Library Collection brings back to life books of enduring scholarly value (including out-of-copyright works originally issued by other publishers) across a wide range of disciplines in the humanities and social sciences and in science and technology.

The Origin of Printing

In Two Essays

WILLIAM BOWYER

CAMBRIDGE
UNIVERSITY PRESS

University Printing House, Cambridge, CB2 8BS, United Kingdom

Cambridge University Press is part of the University of Cambridge.

It furthers the University's mission by disseminating knowledge in the pursuit of
education, learning and research at the highest international levels of excellence.

www.cambridge.org
Information on this title: www.cambridge.org/9781108073837

© in this compilation Cambridge University Press 2014

This edition first published 1774
This digitally printed version 2014

ISBN 978-1-108-07383-7 Paperback

This book reproduces the text of the original edition. The content and language reflect
the beliefs, practices and terminology of their time, and have not been updated.

Cambridge University Press wishes to make clear that the book, unless originally published
by Cambridge, is not being republished by, in association or collaboration with,
or with the endorsement or approval of, the original publisher or its successors in title.

THE
ORIGIN
OF
PRINTING:
IN TWO ESSAYS:

I. The Subſtance of Dr. MIDDLETON's Diſſertation
on the Origin of Printing in England.

II. Mr. MEERMAN's Account of the Firſt Invention
of the Art.

An APPENDIX is annexed,

1. On the firſt-printed GREEK Books.
2. On the firſt-printed HEBREW Books, with Obſervations
on ſome modern Editions; and a Collation, from WAL-
TON's Polyglott, of a remarkable Paſſage, as printed in
Kings and *Chronicles.*
3. On the early POLYGLOTTS.

LONDON:
Printed for W. BOWYER and J. NICHOLS,
at Cicero's Head, Red-Lion-Paſſage, Fleet-Street.
MDCCLXXIV.

[iii]

ADVERTISEMENT.

THE prefent publication was at firft defigned to have been extended no farther than to re-print the fubftance of Dr. MIDDLETON's Diſſertation, with Remarks on fome miftakes of that ingenious Gentleman; which are thrown into the form of Notes, to diftinguiſh them from the paſſages they are intended to illuftrate. The SECOND ESSAY, though not pretended to be *a complete Hiſtory* of the Origin of the Art, we may venture to aſſert, gives a clearer account of it than any book hitherto publiſhed in this kingdom. It contains, in as concife a manner as poſſible, the fubftance of the *Origines Typographicæ* of the very learned and ingenious Mr. GERARD MEERMAN, Penfionary of Rotterdam; and may be confidered as the outlines of that curious publication, with fupplementary Notes on fome interefting particulars.

Mr. MEERMAN very clearly fixes the firft rudiments of the art to LAURENTIUS, at Harleim; the improvement of it to GEINSFLEICH fenior and his brother GUTENBERG * (aſſiſted by the liberality of FAUSTUS) at Mentz; and the completion of the

* In Engliſh, GOOD-HILL. See PALMER, p. 17.

a 2   whole

whole to PETER SCHOEFFER, in the fame city. The claim of Strasburgh is amply confidered, and evidently overthrown.

Of the APPENDIX, we need only fay, that the affiftance of two valuable Friends has enabled us to make it truly interefting. The Reader will there find a diftinct account of the firft-printed Greek and Hebrew books; a collation of two parallel paffages in the Hebrew Scriptures; and a particular hiftory of the early Polyglotts.

C O N-

C O N T E N T S.

The

vi   C O N T E N T S.

A mif-

---

* In PALMER's Hiftory of Printing, p. 327, mention is
made of a *Book of Mifcellanies*; in the firft leaf of which is
an account of two books printed at St. Alban's, viz. the
Book in which the obfervations are written; and the *Bokys
of Haukyng and Huntyng*, defcribed above, p. 42. Thefe
obfer-

CONTENTS.

obſervations Mr. PALMER has printed, and adds at the end,
" Thus far we have copied from my Lord's manuſcript
" notes." Mr. MEERMAN (vol, I. p. 142) remarks on
this paſſage, " Re penitus examinata, varia ſunt, quæ ean-
" dem narrationem pluſquam ſuſpectam, imo falſam red-
" dant. Primum eſt, quod ipſa annotatio evincat, eam non
" deberi peritiſſimo PEMBROKIÆ Comiti, ut perſuadere
" lectoribus PALMERIUS voluit, ſed alii cuidam anonymo,
" (quippe ſemper in tertia perſona de PEMBROKIÆ Comite
" loquitur, e. g. *as may be ſeen in my Lord's books,* itemque
" *the which my Lord alſo has)* quem ego ipſum PALMERIUM,
" inſignem, dum viveret, impoſtorem, inque ædibus Pem-
" brokianis familiarem fuiſſe ſuſpicor."—I have been informed that an aſſiſtant with PALMER in this work was
PSALMANAZAR, an impoſtor by his own confeſſion. That
he had connexions with PALMER, appears from his Life
written by himſelf, and printed ſince his death. W. B.
1766.

Employed

❖❖❖❖❖❖❖❖❖❖❖

II. Mr. MEERMAN's Account of the Firſt In-
vention of the Art.

There

This

C O N T E N T S.   xi

b 2   More

APPEN-

APPENDIX.

N° I.

Short

Nº II.

On the firſt-printed Hebrew Books; with
Obſervations on ſome modern Editions.

A *pre-*

N° III.

On the firft-printed Polyglotts.

A Poly-

THE

THE

ORIGIN

OF

PRINTING.

WITH REMARKS.

IT was a conftant opinion, delivered down by our
hiftorians, as hath been obferved by Dr. MID-
DLETON, that the ART OF PRINTING was introduced and firft practifed in England by WIL-
LIAM CAXTON, a mercer and citizen of London;
who, by his travels abroad, and a refidence of many
years in Holland, Flanders, and Germany, in the
affairs of trade, had an opportunity of informing
himfelf of the whole method and procefs of the art;
and by the encouragement of the great, and particularly of the abbot of Weftminfter, firft fet up a prefs
in that abbey, and began to print books foon after the
year 1471.

This was the tradition of our writers; till a book,
which had fcarce been obferved before the Reftoration, was then taken notice of by the curious, with
a date of its impreffion from Oxford, anno 1468, and

B   was

was confidered immediately as a clear proof and monument of the exercife of printing in that univerfity,
feveral years before Caxton began to deal in it.

The book, which is in our public library, is a
fmall volume of forty-one leaves in quarto, with this
title: " Expoficio Sancti Jeronimi in Simbolum Apof-
tolorum ad Papam Laurentium:" and at the end,
" Explicit expoficio, &c. Impreffa Oxonie, & finita
Anno Domini M,CCCC,LXVIII. XVII die Decem-
bris."

The appearance of this book has robbed Caxton
of a glory that he had long poffeffed, of being the
author of printing to this kingdom, and Oxford ever
fince carried the honour of the firft prefs. The only
difficulty was, to account for the filence of hiftory in
an event fo memorable, and the want of any memo-
rial in the univerfity itfelf, concerning the eftablifhment of a new art amongft them, of fuch ufe and
benefit to learning. But this likewife has been cleared up, by the difcovery of a record, which had lain
obfcure and unknown at Lambeth houfe, in the Regifter of the See of Canterbury, and gives a narrative of the whole tranfaction, drawn up at the very
time.

An account of this record was firft publifhed in a
thin quarto volume, in Englifh; with this title, " The
Original and Growth of PRINTING, collected out
of Hiftory and the Records of this Kingdome: where-
in is alfo demonftrated, that Printing appertaineth to
the Prerogative Royal; and is a Flower of the Crown
of

of England. By Richard Atkyns, efq.—Whitehall,
April the 25, 1664. By order and appointment of
the right honourable Mr. Secretary Morrice, let this
be printed. THO. RYCAUT. London: Printed by
John Streater, for the Author. 1664." 4to.

It fets forth in fhort [A], " That as foon as the
art of printing made fome noife in Europe, Thomas
Bourchier, archbifhop of Canterbury, moved the
then king (Hen. VI.) to ufe all poffible means for
procuring a printing-mold (for fo it 'twas there called)
to be brought into this kingdom. The king (a good
man, and much given to works of this nature)
readily hearkened to the motion; and taking private
advice, how to effect his defign, concluded it could
not be brought about without great fecrecy, and a
confiderable fum of money given to fuch perfon or
perfons as would draw off fome of the workmen of
Harleim in Holland, where John Cuthenberg had
newly invented it, and was himfelf perfonally at
work. 'Twas refolved, that lefs than one thoufand
marks would not produce the defired effect; towards
which fum the faid archbifhop prefented the king
three hundred marks. The money being now prepared, the management of the defign was committed

[A] Dr. Middleton having given a very fmall extract
from this book of Mr. Atkyns, it was thought proper to
lay the fubftance of it more fully before the reader, in the
words of Mr. Maittaire, Annales Typographicæ, vol. i. p.
28.—Mr. Palmer has alfo printed a particular account of it,
Hift. of Printing, p. 314. B.

to Mr. Robert Turnour; who then was of the robes
to the king, and a perſon moſt in favour with him
of any of his condition. Mr. Turnour took to his
aſſiſtance Mr. Caxton, a citizen of good abilities, who
trading much into Holland, might be a creditable
pretence, as well for his going, as ſtay in the Low
Countries. Mr. Turnour was in diſguiſe (his beard
and hair ſhaven quite off); but Mr. Caxton appeared
known and public. They, having received the ſaid
ſum of one thouſand marks, went firſt to Amſterdam,
then to Leyden, not daring to enter Harleim itſelf;
for the town was very jealous, having impriſoned
and apprehended divers perſons, who came from
other parts for the ſame purpoſe. They ſtaid, till
they had ſpent the whole one thouſand marks in gifts
and expences: ſo as the king was fain to ſend five
hundred marks more, Mr. Turnour having written to
the king, that he had almoſt done his work; a bar-
gain (as he ſaid) being ſtruck betwixt him and two
Hollanders, for bringing off one of the under-work-
men, whoſe name was Frederick Corſells (or rather
Corſellis), who late one night ſtoie from his fellows
in diſguiſe into a veſſel prepared before for that purpoſe; and ſo the wind, favouring the deſign, brought
him ſafe to London. 'Twas not thought ſo prudent
to ſet him on work at London: but by the archbiſhop's means (who had been vice-chancellor and afterwards chancellor of the univerſity of Oxon) Corſellis
was carried with a guard to Oxon; which guard
conſtantly watched to prevent Corſellis from any poſſible

ble efcape, till he had made good his promife in teaching them how to print. So that at Oxford printing was firft fet up in England, which was before there was any printing-prefs or printer in France, Spain, Italy, or Germany (except the city of Mentz), which claims feniority, as to printing, even of Harleim itfelf, calling her city, " Urbem Moguntinam artis typographicæ inventricem primam," though 'tis known to be otherwife; that city gaining that art by the brother of one of the workmen of Harleim, who had learnt it at home of his brother, and after fet up for himfelf at Mentz [B]. This prefs at Oxon was at leaft ten years before there was any printing in Europe, except at Harleim and Mentz, where it was but new born. This prefs at Oxford was afterwards found inconvenient, to be the fole printing-place of England; as being too far from London and the fea. Wherefore the king fet up a prefs at St. Alban's, and another in the city of Weftminfter;

[B] This circumftance is urged as a great confirmation of the authority of this narration. The fact here afferted ha been proved to be true, viz. that there were two brothers, JOHN GEINSFLEISCH fenior and junior, who practifed this art on feparate wooden types, firft at Harleim, and that the latter carried it to Mentz. This opinion is fo contrary to what all the Englifh hiftorians relate, as Fabian, Hollingfhed, Stow, Baker, &c. and Caxton himfelf, that the author muft have had his information from fome one who had it from the moft authentic monuments. MEERMAN, vol. ii. p. 30.

where

where they printed feveral books of *divinity* and *phyfic*; *for the king* (for reafons beft known to himfelf and council) *permitted then no law-books to be printed*; nor did any printer exercife that art, but only fuch as were the king's fworn fervants; *the king himfelf having the price and emolument for printing books.*—By this means the art grew fo famous, that anno primo Ric. III. c. 9, when an act of parliament was made for reftraint of aliens from ufing any handicrafts here (except as fervants to natives), a fpecial provifo was inferted, that ftrangers might bring in printed or written books, to fell at their pleafure, and exercife the art of printing here, notwithftanding that act: fo in that fpace of forty or fifty years, by the indulgence of Edward IV, Edward V, Richard III, Henry VII, and Henry VIII, the Englifh proved fo good proficients in printing, and grew fo numerous, as to furnifh the kingdom with books; and fo fkilful, as to print them as well as any beyond the feas; as appears by the act 25 Henry VIII, cap. 15, which abrogates the faid provifo for that reafon.   And it was further enacted in the faid ftatute, that if any perfon bought foreign books bound, he fhould pay 6*s.* 8*d.* per book.   And it was further provided and enacted, that in cafe the faid printers or fellers of books were unreafonable in their prices, they fhould be moderated by the lord chancellor, lord treafurer, the two lords chief juftices, or any two of them; who alfo had power to fine them 3*s.* 4*d.* for every book, whofe price fhall be

enhanced.

enhanced.—But when they were by charter corpora‑
ted with *book-binders*, *book-fellers*, and *founders of
letters*, 3 and 4 Philip and Mary, and called THE
COMPANY OF STATIONERS—they kickt againſt the
power that gave them life, &c.—Queen Elizabeth,
the firſt year of her reign, grants by patent *the pri‑
vilege of ſole printing all books that touch or con‑
cern the common laws of England*, to Tottel a ſer‑
vant to her majeſty, who kept it intire to his death;
after him, to one Yeſt Weirt, another ſervant to her
majeſty; after him, to Weight and Norton; and af
ter them, king James grants the ſame privilege to
More, one of the ſignet; which grant continues to
this day, &c."

From the authority of this record, (ſays Dr. M.) all
our later writers declare Corſellis to be the firſt printer
in England; Mr. Anthony Wood, the learned Mr.
Mattaire, Palmer, and one Bagford, an induſtrious man,
who had publiſhed propoſals for an Hiſtory of Print‑
ing, and whoſe manuſcript papers were communicated
to me by my worthy and learned friend Mr. Baker:
but it is ſtrange that a piece ſo fabulous, and carry‑
ing ſuch evident marks of forgery, could impoſe upon
men ſo knowing and inquiſitive.

For firſt; the faft is laid quite wrong as to time;
near the end of Henry the Sixth's reign, in the very
heat of the civil wars; when it is not credible that a
prince, ſtruggling for life as well as his crown, ſhould
have leiſure or diſpoſition to attend to a projeft that
could hardly be thought of, much leſs executed, in
times

times of fuch calamity [C]. The printer, it is faid, was gracioufly received by the king, made one of his fworn fervants, and fent down to Oxford with a guard, &c. all which muft have paffed before the year MCCCCLIX : for Edward IV, was proclaimed in London, in the end of it, according to our computation, on the 4th of March, and crowned about the Midfummer following (fee Caxton's Chronicle) [D]; and

[C] But this king, after he had laid the foundations for two of the greateft feminaries of literature in England, Eaton and King's College, Cambridge, beftowed his royal munificence to two colleges in Oxford, amidft all his troubles. MEERMAN, vol. ii. p. 32.

[D] Whatever Caxton's Chronicle may fay, we have a much greater authority for fixing the beginning of king Edward's reign in MCCCCLX-I, i. e, a year later than Dr. Middleton does. The firft inftrument in Rymer's Conventiones, &c. in this king's reign, begins thus; " Mem. quod die Martis, decimo die Martii, anno regni regis Edw. primo." Now in the year MCCCCLX-I, the tenth of March fell upon a Tuefday; but in MCCCCLIX-LX, on a Monday. This miftake indeed of Dr. Middleton's is happily a confirmation of his own hypothefis. A tranfpofition of a numeral in Caxton's Chronicle (Mar. MCCCCLIX for MCCCCLXI) made him antedate the reign of Edward IV ; as the omiffion of x in the Expofitio Hieronymi, printed at Oxford, is fuppofed to have made the public antedate the beginning of printing there. But that Univerfity needs no fuch fupport: though Dr. M. does; who left this miftake in the edition of his works, publifhed in 1752, vol iii. p. 231, 4to. though it had been pointed out, as above, in the Grubftreet Journal, N°. 273, March 20, 1735. B,

yet

yet we have no fruit of all this labour and expence till ten years after, when the little book, defcribed above, is fuppofed to have been publifhed from that prefs.

Secondly; the filence of Caxton, concerning a fact in which he is faid to be a principal actor, is a fufficient confutation of it: for it was a conftant cuftom with him, in the prefaces or conclufions of his works, to give an hiftorical account of all his labours and tranfactions, as far as they concerned the publifhing and printing of books. And, what is ftill ftronger, in The Continuation of the Polychronicon, compiled by himfelf, and carried down to the end of Henry the Sixth's reign, he makes no mention of the expedition in queft of a Printer; which he could not have omitted had it been true: whilft in the fame book he takes notice of the invention and beginning of Printing in the city of Mentz [E]; which I fhall make fome ufe of by and by.

There is a further circumftance in Caxton's hiftory, that feems inconfiftent with the record; for we find
him

[E] As Caxton makes no mention in his Polychronicon of his *expedition in queft of a Printer*; fo neither does he of his bringing the art firft into England, which it is as much a wonder he fhould omit as the other. And as to his faying that *the invention of Printing was at Mentz*, he means, of printing on *fufile* feparate types. In this he copies, as many others have, from the *Fafciculus temporum*; a work

C   written

him ſtill beyond ſea, about twelve years after the
ſuppoſed tranſaction, " learning with great charge
and trouble the art of printing ;" (Recule of the
Hiſtories of Troye, in the end of the 2d and 3d
books ;) which he might have done with eaſe at
home, if he had got Corſellis into his hands, as the
record imports, ſo many years before : but he probably learnt it at Cologn, where he reſided in 1471,

written in 1470, by WERNERUS ROLEVINCH DE LAER,
a Carthuſian Monk, a Mſ. copy of which was in the library
of Gerard Jo. Voſſius (ſee lib. iii. *de Hiſtor. Latin.* c. 6) ;
and afterwards continued to the year 1474, when it was firſt
printed at Cologn, *typis Arnoldi ter Huernen.* It was re-pub-
liſhed in 1481, by HEINRICUS WIRCZBURG DE VACH, a
Cluniac monk, without mentioning the name either of the
printer or of the place of publication. We are told, indeed, in
a colophon, that the book was publiſhed *ſub Lodovico Gruerie
Comite magnifico* ; but, as the country whence this illuſtrious
nobleman aſſumed his title was unknown to the learned editor of the *Origines Typographicæ,* it will be no eaſy taſk for an
Engliſhman to diſcover it : nor is it of much conſequence ;
as this edition, though ſomewhat enlarged, was miſerably in-
terpolated throughout, and particularly ſo in the account of
the invention of Printing.—It is plain, however, that Caxton
had one at leaſt, or more probably both of theſe editions before him, when he wrote his continuation of the *Polychronicon,*
as he mentions this work in his preface, and adopts the ſen-
timents of its editor. (See MEERMAN, vol. ii. p. 37. and
his *Documenta,* Nº VII, XXIV, and XXV.) N.

(Recule,

(Recule, &c. ibid.), and whence books had been firſt printed with date, the year before [F].

To the ſilence of Caxton, we may add that of the Dutch writers: for it is very ſtrange, as Mr. Chevillier obſerves, if the ſtory of the record be true, " That Adrian Junius, who has collected all the groundleſs ones that favour the pretenſions of Harleim, ſhould never have heard of it." (L'Origine de l'Imprimerie de Paris, c. i. p. 25.)

[F] Caxton tells us, in the preface to *The Hiſtory of Troye*, that he began that tranſlation March 1, 1468, at Bruges; that he proceeded on with it at Ghent; that he finiſhed it at Cologn, 1471; and printed it, probably, in that city with his own types. He was thirty years abroad, chiefly in Holland; and lived in the court of Margaret ducheſs of Burgundy, fiſter of our Edward IV. It was therefore much eaſier to print his book at Cologn, than to croſs the ſea to learn the art at Oxford. But further, there was a ſpecial occaſion for his printing it abroad. Corſellis had brought over ſo far the art of printing as he had learnt it at Harleim, which was the method of printing on *wooden ſeparate* types, having the face of the letter cut upon them. But the art of *caſting* types being divulged in 1462 by the workmen of Mentz, he thought proper to learn that advantageous branch before he returned to England. This method of caſting the types was ſuch an improvement, that they looked on it as the *original* of printing; and Caxton, as moſt others do, aſcribes that to *Mentz*.—Caxton was an aſſiſtant with Turner in getting off *Corſellis*; but it is no where ſuppoſed that he came with him into *England*. See MEERMAN, vol. ii. p. 34. B.

C 2 But

But thirdly ; the moſt direct and internal proof of its forgery, is its aſcribing the origin of Printing to Harleim ; " where John Guttemberg, the inventor, is ſaid to have been perſonally at work when Corſellis was brought away, and the art itſelf to have been firſt carried to Mentz by a brother of one of Guttemberg's workmen [G] :" for it is certain beyond all doubt, that Printing was firſt invented and propagated from Mentz. Caxton's teſtimony ſeems alone to be deciſive ; who, in the Continuation of the Polychronicon, fol. 433 [H], ſays, " About this time (viz. anno 1455) the crafte of emprynting was firſt found in Mogounce in Almayne, &c." He was abroad in the very country, and at the time, when the firſt project and thought of it began, and the rudeſt eſſays of it were attempted ; where he continued for thirty years, viz. from 1441 to 1471 : and, as he was particularly curious and inquiſitive after this new art, of which he was endeavouring to get a perfect information, he could not be ignorant of the place where it was firſt exerciſed. This confutes what Palmer conjectures, to confirm the credit of the record, " That the compiler might take up with the common report, that paſſed current at the time in Holland, in favour of Harleim ; or probably re-

[G] See the words of the record as printed above, .p. 5.

[H] The teſtimony of Caxton will perhaps not appear ſo very DECISIVE as Dr. M. imagines, if the circumſtances mentioned above, in the note [E], p. 9, 10, are candidly conſidered. N.

ceive it from Caxton himfelf;" (Hift. of Printing, book iii. p. 318 :) for it does not appear that there was any fuch report at the time, nor many years after; and Caxton, we fee, was better informed from his own knowledge ; and, had Palmer been equally curious, he could not have been ignorant of this teftimony of his in the very cafe.

Befides the evidence of Caxton, we have another contemporary authority, from the Black Book, or Regifter of the Garter, publifhed by Mr. Anftis, where, in the thirty-fifth year of Henry VI, anno 1457, it is faid, " In this year of our moft pious king, the art of printing bookes firft began at Mentz, a famous city of Germany." Hift. of Garter, vol. ii. p. 161.

Fabian likewife, the writer of the Chronicle, an author of good credit, who lived at the fame time with Caxton, though fome years younger, fays, " This yere, (viz. 35 Henry VI,) after the opynyon of dyverfe wryters, began in a citie of Almaine, namyd Mogunce, the crafte of empryntynge bokys, which fen that tyme hath had wonderful encreace." Thefe three teftimonies have not been produced before, that I know of ; two of them were communicated to me by Mr. Baker, who of all men is the moft able, as well as the moft willing, to give information in every point of curious and uncommon hiftory.

I need not purfue this queftion any farther ; the teftimonies commonly alledged in it may be feen in Mr. Mattaire, Palmer, &c. I fhall only obferve, that
we

14 THE ORIGIN

we have full and authentic evidence for the caufe of Mentz, in an edition of Livy from that place, anno 1518, by John Scheffer, the fon of Peter, the partner and fon-in-law of John Fauſt : where the PATENT OF PRIVILEGE GRANTED BY THE EMPEROR TO THE PRINTER; the prefatory epiſtle of Erafmus; the epiſtle dedicatory to the prince by Ulrich Hutten; the epiſtle to the reader of the two learned men who had the care of the edition; all concur in aſſerting the origin of the art to that city, and the invention and firſt exerciſe of it to Fauſt : and Erafmus particularly, who was a Dutchman, would not have *decided againſt* [I] his

own

[I] It muſt be allowed that the edition of Livy (which, by the bye, Dr. Middleton has antedated, it being publiſhed in 1519) is indeed *a full and authentic evidence for the caufe of Mentz.* The feveral authorities Dr. Middleton has referred to are preferved by Mr. Meerman, in his *Documenta,* N° XLVII. The emperor's patent, dated Dec. 9, 1518, begins thus : " MAXIMILIANUS, &c. honeſto noſtro, & facri Imperii fideli nobis dilecto JOHANNI SCHEFFER, Chalchógrapho Moguntino, gratiam noſtram Cæſaream, & omne bonum. Cum, ficut docti & moniti fumus fide dignorum teſtimonio, ingeniofum Chalcographiæ, AUTHORE AVO TUO, inventum, felicibus incrementis, in univerfum orbem promanaverit, &c." It is faid by ULRICH HUTTEN, in the dedication to *Albert* the archbiſhop, " Si vel locum voluit LIVIUS aliquem fuo decorare egreſſu, quem debuit urbi, ARTIS omnium, quæ uſque funt, aut unquam fuerunt, PRÆSTANTISSIMÆ INVENTRICI ac ALUMNÆ (IMPRESSORIAM puto, quam hæc dedit) præferre ?"—In the epiſtle to the reader by NICHOLAS CARBACHIUS,

own country, had there been any ground for the claim of Harleim.

But to return to the Lambeth record: as it was *never heard of before the publication of Atkins's book*, so it has never since been seen or produced by any man; though the Registers of Canterbury have on many occasions been diligently and particularly searched for it. They were examined without doubt very carefully by archbishop Parker, for the compiling his Antiquities of the British Church; where, in the life of Thomas Bourchier, though he congratulates that age on the noble and useful invention of

BACHIUS, Jo. SCHEFFER is mentioned as "Chalcographus, à cujus avo Chalcographe IN HAC PRIMUM URBE INVENTA exercitaque est." ERASMUS's words are, "Quorum princeps fuisse FERTUR JOHANNES FAUST, avus ejus, cui LIVIUM hunc debemus; ut hoc egregium decus partim ad JOHANNEM SCHEFFER, velut *hereditario jure* devolvatur, partim ad MOGUNTIACÆ civitatis gloriam pertineat." And Fabian, before him, says, AFTER THE OPINION OF DIVERSE WRITERS. So that it is probable there was *some report* (whether upon Harleim's claiming the honour of printing on wooden types first, or not) that Mentz was not the place where Printing was first invented, though the united force of the above authentic testimonies might seem to confirm its claim to that honour —It may be nearer the truth, if we suppose (to apply the words of ULRICH HUTTEN a little differently from his intentions) that HARLEIM was the *inventrix*, and *Mentz* the *alumna* of PRINTING; though the improvements made in the art by the latter were so very considerable, as to deserve the name of a new invention. N.

Printing,

Printing, yet he is filent as to the introduction of it into England by the endeavours of that archbifhop; nay, his giving the honour of the invention to Straf- burg, clearly fhews that he knew nothing of the ftory of Corfellis conveyed from Harleim, and that the record was not in being in his time. Palmer himfelf owns, "That it is not to be found there now; for that the late earl of Pembroke affured him, that he had employed a perfon for fome time to fearch for it, but in vain." Hift. of Printing, p. 314.

On thefe grounds we may pronounce the record to be a forgery; though all the writers above-mentioned take pains to fupport its credit, and call it an authen- tic piece.

Atkins, who by his manner of writing feems to have been *a bold and vain man*, might poffibly be *the inventor*; for he had an intereft in impofing it upon the world, in order to confirm the argument of his book, that *Printing was of the Prerogative Royal*; in oppofition to the *Company of Stationers*, with whom he was engaged in an expenfive fuit of law, in de- fence of the *King's Patents*, under which he claimed *fome exclufive powers of Printing*. For he tells us, p. 3, "That, upon confidering the thing, he could not but think that a public perfon, more eminent than a mercer, and a public purfe, muft needs be con- cerned in fo public a good: and the more he confider- ed, the more inquifitive he was to find out the truth." So that he had formed his hypothefis before he had found his record; which he publifhed, he fays, "as a friend

a friend to truth ; not to suffer one man to be entitled
to the worthy atchievements of another; and as a
friend to himself, not to lose one of his best argu-
ments of entitling the King to this Art." But, if Atkins was not himself the contriver, he was imposed
upon at least by some more crafty ; who imagined
that his interest in the cause, and the warmth that he
shewed in prosecuting it, would induce him to swallow
for genuine, whatever was offered of the kind [K].

We

[K] On the other hand, is it likely that Mr. Atkins would
dare to *forge* a record to be laid before the king and council,
and which his adversaries, with whom he was at law, could
disprove ? (2.) He says he received this history from a person of honour, who was some time keeper of the Lambeth
Library. It was easy to have confuted this evidence, if it
was false, when he published it, Apr. 25, 1664. (3.) John
Bagford (who was born in England 1651, and might know
Mr. Atkins, who died 1677), in his History of Printing at Oxford, blames those who doubted of the authenticity of the
Lambeth Mf. ; and tells us that he knew Sir John Birkenhead
had an authentic copy of it, when in 1665 [which Bagford
by some mistake calls 1664, and is followed in it by Meer-
man] he was appointed by the house of commons to draw
up a bill relating to the exercise of that art. This is confirmed by the Journals of that house, Friday, Oct. 27, 1665,
vol. VIII. p. 622 ; where it is ordered that this Sir John Birkenhead should carry the bill on that head to the house of
lords, for their consent.—The act was agreed to in the upper
house on Tuesday Oct. 31, and received the royal assent on
the same day ; immediately after which, the parliament was
prorogued. See Journals of the House of Lords, Vol. XI.

D   p. 700.

We have now cleared our hands of the record; but the book stands firm, as a monument of the exercise

p. 700.—It is probable then that, after Mr. Atkins had published his book in April 1664, the parliament thought proper, the next year, to inquire into *the right of the* KING's PREROGATIVE; and that Sir John Birkenhead took care to infpect the original, then in the custody of Archbifhop Sheldon : and finding it not fufficient to prove what Mr. Atkins had cited it for, made no report of the Mf. to the house; but only moved, that the former law fhould be renewed. — The Mf. was probably never returned to the proper keeper of it; and was afterwards burnt in the fire of London, Sept. 13, 1666. (4.) That Printing was practifed at Oxford, was a prevailing opinion long before Atkins. Bryan Twyne, in his *Apologia pro Antiquitate Academiæ Oxonienfis*, publifhed 1608, tells us it is fo delivered down in *ancient writings; having heard probably of this Lambeth Mf.* And king Charles I, in his letters patent to the Univerfity of Oxford, 5 Mar. in the eleventh of his reign, 1635, mentions Printing as brought to *Oxford* from abroad —As to what is objected, "that it is not likely that prefs fhould undergo a ten or eleven years fleep, viz. from 1468 to 1479," it is probably urged without foundation. Corfellis might print feveral books without date or name of the place, as Ulric Zell did at Cologn, from 1467 to 1473, and from that time to 1494. Corfellis's name, it may be faid, appears not in any of his publications; nor does that of Joannes Peterfhemius. See MEERMAN, vol. I. p. 34; vol. II. p. 21—27, &c.

Further, the famous SHAKESPEARE, who was born in 1564, and died 1616, in the Second Part of Henry VI.

Act

ercife of printing in Oxford fix years older than any book of Caxton with date. The fact is ftrong, and what

Act iv. Sc. 7, introduces the rebel *John Cade*, thus upbraiding Lord Treafurer SAY: " Thou haft moft traiteroufly corrupted the youth of the realm, in creating a grammar-fchool; and whereas before, our forefathers had no other book but the fcore and the tally, thou haft caufed PRINTING to be ufed; and, contrary to the king, his crown, and dignity, thou haft built a paper-mill."—Whence now had Shakefpeare this accufation againft Lord SAY? We are told in the Poetical Regifter, vol. II. p. 231. ed. Lond. 1724, that it was from FABIAN, POL. VERGIL, HALL, HOLLINGSHED, GRAFTON, STOW, SPEED, &c. But not one of thefe afcribes Printing to the reign of Henry VI. On the contrary, Stow, in his Annals, printed at London, 1560, p. 686, gives it exprefsly to William Caxton, 1471. " The noble fcience of Printing was about this time found in Germany at Magunce, by one John Guthemburgus a knight. One Conradus an Almaine brought it into Rome: William Caxton of London mercer brought it into England about the yeare 1471, and firft practifed the fame in the Abbie of St. Peter at Weftminfter; after which time it was likewife practifed in the Abbies of St. Auguftine at Canturburie, Saint Albons, and other monafteries of England." What then fhall we fay, that the above is an anachronifm arbitrarily put into the mouth of an ignorant fellow out of Shakefpeare's head? I could believe fo, but that we have the record of Mr. Atkins confirming the fame in K. Charles the Second's time. Shall we fay, that Mr. Atkins borrowed the ftory from Shakefpeare, and publifhed it with fome improvements of money laid out by Henry VI; from whence it

might

what in ordinary cafes paffes for certain evidence of
the age of books; but in this, there are fuch contrary
facts to balance it, and fuch circumftances to turn the

might be received by Charles II, as a prerogative of the
crown ? But this is improbable, fince Shakefpeare makes
Lord Treafurer SAY the inftrument of importing it, of whom
Mr. Atkins mentions not a word. Another difference there
will ftill be between Shakefpeare and the Lambeth Mf.; the
Poet placing it before 1449, in which year Lord SAY was
beheaded; the Mf. between 1454 and 1459, when Bourchier was Archbifhop,—We muft fay then, that Lord SAY
firft laid the fcheme, and fent fome one to Harleim, though
without fuccefs; but after fome years it was attempted happily by Bourchier. And we muft conclude, that as the ge-
nerality of writers have overlooked the invention of Printing at Harleim with *wooden* types, and have afcribed it to
Mentz where *metal* types were firft made ufe of; fo in England they have paffed by Corfellis (or the firft *Oxford Printer*,
whoever he was, fee the note [P], p. 24), who printed with
wooden types at Oxford, and only mentioned Caxton, as the
original artift who printed with *metal* types at Weftminfter.
See MEERMAN, vol. II. p, vii, viii.—It is ftrange that the
learned Commentators on our great Dramatic Poet, who are
fo minutely particular upon lefs important occafions, fhould
every one of them, Dr. JOHNSON excepted, pafs by this
curious paffage, leaving it entirely unnoticed. And how has
Dr. JOHNSON trifled, by flightly remarking, that "SHAKE-
SPEARE is a little TOO EARLY with this accufation!"—The
great Critic had undertaken to decypher obfolete words, and
inveftigate unintelligible phrafes; but never, perhaps, beftowed a thought on Caxton or Corfellis, on Mr. Atkins or
the authenticity of the Lambeth Record. B. & N.

fcale,

scale, that, to speak my mind freely, I take the date in queftion to have been falfified originally by the printer, either by defign or miftake, and an x to have been dropt or omitted in the age of its impreffion.

Examples of the kind are common in the Hiftory of Printing. I have obferved feveral dates altered very artfully after publication, to give them the credit of greater antiquity. They have at Harleim, in large quarto, a tranflation into Dutch of *Bartholomæus de proprietatibus rerum,* printed *anno* MCCCCXXXV, by Jacob Bellart: this they fhew to confirm their claim to the earlieft printing, and deceive the unfkilful. But Mr. Bagford, who had feen another copy with a true date, difcovered the cheat; by which the L had been erafed fo cunningly, that it was not eafy to perceive it [L]. But befides the frauds of an after-contrivance, there are many falfe dates originally given by the printers; partly through defign, to

[L] See Mr. Bagford's Papers.—Mr. Maittaire, Annal. Typogr. tom. I. p. 190, mentions an edition of this book at Cologn in MCCCCLXX. The copy which this gentleman had feen was in the earl of Oxford's library, and came afterwards into the hands of Mr. T. Ofborn; in whofe Catalogues it frequently appeared, with the date MCCCCLXX. Mr. Meerman, who was convinced that this date muft either be a miftake or an impofition, had the curiofity (when, in 1759, he refided in London in a public capacity) to examine Mr. Ofborn's book; which proved to be the edition of MCCCCLXXXIII (which Mr. Maittaire has alfo taken notice of), with the four laft numerals very artfully erafed. See MEERMAN, vol. I. p. 59. N.

raife

raife the value of their works, but chiefly through negligence and blunder. There is a Bible at Augfburg, of the year 1449, where the two laft figures are tranf-pofed, and fhould ftand thus, 1494: Chevillier (Orig. de l'Imprim. de Paris, c. v. p. 96.) mentions three more ; one at Paris of 1443 ; another at Lyons, 1446 ; a third at Bafil, 1450; though Printing was not ufed in any of thefe places till many years after, Orlandi defcribes three books with the like miftake from Mentz : and Jo. Koelhoff, who firft printed about the year 1470, at Cologn, has dated one of his books anno MCCCC. with a c omitted ; and another, anno 1458; which Palmer (Hift. of Printing, p. 179) imputes to defign, rather than miftake [M].

But

[M] Mr. Meerman, after fixing the invention of Printing beyond a doubt *in the fifteenth century*, takes notice of a Ger-man tract, *von dem Cyrurgus*, 1397. This, he obferves, and fome other fimilar inftances, may beyond a doubt be pro-nounced A FORGERY ; and there will be little danger of a miftake, if we extend this affertion to all books in general that have an earlier date than MCCCCLVII, when the *Pfalter* was publifhed at Mentz, which is the firft work that is known to have a date to it. See Maittaire, Annal. Typogr. tom. I. p. 2. Marchand, Hift. de l'Imprim. p. 113. Nau-dæus, Addit. à l'Hift. de Louis XI. p. 110.—Some writers have afcribed the origin of Printing to the Eaft, and affixed a much earlier period to its invention, particularly P. Jovius, Hift. lib. xiv. p. 226. ed. Florent. 1550, from whom Ofo-rius and many others have embraced the fame opinion. But thefe have evidently confounded the European mode of

PRINTING

But what is moft to our point, is a book from the famous printer, Nicolas Jenfon; of which Mr. Maittaire gave the firft notice, called Decor Puellarum; printed anno MCCCCLXI. All the other works of Jenfon were publifhed from Venice between the years MCCCCLXX and MCCCCLXXX; which juftly raifed a fufpicion, that an x had been dropt from the date of this, which ought to be advanced ten years forward; fince it was not credible, that fo great a mafter of the art, who at once invented and perfected it, could lie fo many years idle and unemployed. The fufpicion appeared to be well grounded, from an edition of Tully's Epiftles at Venice, *the firft work of another famed printer, John de Spira, anno* MCCCCLXIX [N]; who, in the four following verfes, at the end of the book, claims the honour of being the firft who had printed in that city:

PRINTING with the *engraved tablets* which to this day are ufed in China. The invention of thefe tablets has been afcribed by many writers even to an earlier period than the commencement of the Chriftian æra; but is with more probability affigned, by the very accurate PHIL. COUPLET, to the year 930. The *Hiftoria Sinenfis* of ABDALLA, written in Perfic in 1317, fpeaks of it as an art in very common ufe. See MEERMAN, vol. I. p. 16, 218, 219; vol. II. p. 186. N.

[N] And yet in the Catalogue of the Harleian Library, vol. III. p. 231, a book is mentioned as printed at Venice a year before this of John de Spira, viz. *Fr. Maturantii de componendis verfibus Hexametro et Pentametro, by Ranolt.*— Venet. 1468. B.

" Primus

"Primus in Adriaca formis impreffit aënis
Urbe libros Spirâ genitus de ftirpe Johannes.
In reliquis fit quanta, vides, fpes, lector, habenda,
Quum labor hic primus calamis fuperaverit artem."

It is, I know, the more current opinion, confirmed by the teftimony of contemporary writers, that *Jenfon was the firft printer at Venice* [O]: But thefe verfes of John de Spira, publifhed *at the time*, as well as *the place*, in which they both lived, and *in the face of his rival Jenfon*, without any contradiction from him, feem to have a weight too great to be over-ruled by any foreign evidence whatfoever.

But whilft I am now writing, an unexpected inftance is fallen into my hands, to the fupport of my opinion; an *Inauguration Speech of the Woodwardian Profeffor, Mr. Mafon*, juft frefh from the prefs, with its date given ten years earlier than it fhould have been, by the omiffion of an x, viz. MDCCXXIV; and the very blunder exemplified in the laft piece printed at Cambridge, which I fuppofe to have happened in the firft from Oxford [P].

Thefe

[O] Maittaire, Annal. Typ. tom. I. p. 36, &c. It. Append. ad tom. I. p. 5, 6.

[P] The following curious remarks, on this paffage of Dr. Middleton, appeared in The Weekly Mifcellany, Saturday, April 26, 1735, in a letter figned OXONIDES: "I think the learned author has fufficiently expofed the idle ftory of FREDERICK CORSELLIS, and entirely concur with him

Thefe inftances, with many more that might be collected, fhew the poffibility of my conjecture; and, for

him in rejecting it. But when he compliments CAXTON with the name of our Firft Printer, notwithftanding the authority of a book printed at *Oxford,* and dated in the year MCCCCLXVIII, I cannot go fo far with him. We fhould not pretend to fet afide the authority of *a plain date,* without very ftrong and cogent reafons; and I am afraid what the Doctor has in this cafe advanced will not appear, on examination, to carry that weight with it that he feems to imagine. There may be, and have been, miftakes and forgeries in the date both of books and of records too; but this is never allowed as a reafon for fufpecting fuch as bear no mark of either. We cannot, from a blunder in the laft book printed at Cambridge, infer the like blunder in the firft book printed at Oxford. Befides, the *type* ufed in this our Oxford edition feems to be no fmall proof of its antiquity. It is the *German* letter, and very nearly the fame with that ufed by FUST [who has been fuppofed to be] the firft Printer; whereas CAXTON and ROOD ufe a quite different letter, fomething between this *German* and our old *Englifh* letter, which was foon after introduced by DE WORDE and PYNSON. Laftly, the fuppofed year of this edition is much about the time that the printers at Mentz difperfed, and carried the art of Printing with them to moft parts of Europe. This circumftance, joined to that of the letter, inclines me to think, *that one of thefe printers might then come over to England, and follow his profeffion at Oxford.* Thefe, I muft own, are only conjectural proofs, nor can we expect any other in the prefent cafe. We find moft points of antiquity involved in obfcurity; and, what is not

E   a little

for the probability of it, the book itfelf affords fufficient proof: For, not to infift on what is lefs material, the *neatnefs of the letter, and regularity of the
page,* &c. above thofe of Caxton ; it has one mark,
that feems to carry the matter beyond probable, and
to make it even certain, viz, *the ufe of fignatures,* or
letters of the alphabet placed at the bottom of the
page, to fhew the fequel of the page and leaves of
each book : an improvement contrived for the direction of the bookbinders; which yet was not practifed or invented at the time when this book is fup-

a little furprizing, the Art of Printing, which has given light
to moft other things, hides its own head in darknefs.—But
our ingenious Differtator feems to think his proofs attended
with more certainty. Let us then examine what he fays:
And firft, the neatnefs of the letter, and the regularity
of the page, prove, if any thing, the very reverfe of what
the Doctor afferts. The art of Printing was almoft in its
infancy brought to perfection, but afterwards debafed by
later printers, who confulted rather the cheapnefs, than the
neatnefs of their work. Our learned Differtator cannot be
unacquainted with the labours of FUST and JENSON. He
muft know, that though other printers may have printed
more correctly, yet fcarce any excell them, either in the
neatnefs of the letter, or the regularity of the page. The
fame may be obferved in our Englifh printers. CAXTON
and ROOD were indifferently good printers : DE WORDE and
PYNSON were worfe; and thofe that follow them moft abo-
minable. This our *anonymous Oxford Printer* excells them
all ; and for this very reafon I fhould judge him to be the
moft ancient of all." N.

                                           pofed

pofed to be printed: for we find no fignatures in the
books of Fauft or Scheffer at Mentz; nor in the improved or beautiful impreffions of John de Spira, and
Jenfon, at Venice, till feveral years later. We have
a book in our library, that feems to fix the very time
of their invention, at leaft in Venice; the place where
the art itfelf received the greateft improvements: *Baldi
lectura fuper Codic.* &c. printed by John de Colonia
and *Jo. Manthen de Gherretzem, anno* MCCCCLXXIIII:
it is a large and fair volume in folio, *without fignatures,* till about the middle of the book, in which
they are firft introduced, and fo continued forward:
which makes it probable, that the firft thought
of them was fuggefted during the impreffion;
for we have likewife *Lectura Bartholi fuper Codic.*
&c. in two noble and beautiful volumes in folio,
printed the year before at the fame place, by Vin-
delin de Spira, without them: yet from this time
forward they are generally found in all the works of
the Venetian printers, and from them propagated to
the other printers of Europe. They were ufed at Co-
logne, in 1475; at Paris, 1476; by Caxton, not
before 1480: but if the difcovery had been brought
into England and practifed at Oxford twelve years
before, it is not probable that he would have printed
fo long at Weftminfter without them [Q].

Mr.

[Q] Dr. Middleton is miftaken in the time and place of
the invention of fignatures. They are to be found even in

Mr. Palmer indeed tells us, p. 180, 54, that Anthony Zarot was efteemed the inventor of fignatures;
                                                    and

very ancient Mff. which the earlieft printers very ftudioufly
imitated; and they were ufed in fome editions from the
office of Laurence Cofter (from whence Corfellis came),
which confifted of wooden cuts; as in *Figuræ typicæ et anti-
typicæ Novi Teftamenti*: and in fome editions of the metal
letters, as in *Gafp. Pergamenfis epiftolæ*, publifhed at Paris,
without a date, but printed A. D. 1470; (Maittaire, Annal.
vol. I. p. 25;) and in *Mammetrectus*, printed by Helias de
Llouffen, at Bern in Switzerland, 1470; and in *De
Tondeli vifione*, at Antwerp, 1472. Venice, therefore, was
not the place where they were firft introduced.—They began to be ufed in Baldus, it feems, when the book was half
finifhed. The printer of that book might not know, or
did not think, of the ufe of them before. See MEERMAN,
vol. II. p. 28; and Phil. Tranf. vol. XXIII. N° 208.
p. 1509, — OXONIDES fays, " Our Differtator lays great
ftrefs on the ufe of fignatures. But I am afraid no certain
conclufion can be drawn either from the ufe or non-ufe of
thefe leffer improvements of Printing. They have in different places come in ufe at different times, and have not
been continued regularly even at the fame places. If Anthony Zarot ufed them at Milan in 1470, it is certain later
printers there did not follow his example; and the like
might happen alfo in England. But what is more full to
our purpofe, we have in the Bodleian library an Æfop's
Fables printed by Caxton. This is, I believe, the firft book
which has *the leaves numbered.* But yet this improvement,
though more ufeful than that of the fignatures, was difufed
both by Caxton himfelf, and other later printers in Eng-
                                                     land.

and that they are found in a Terence printed by him at Milan in the year 1470, in which he firſt printed. I have not ſeen that Terence; and can only ſay, that I have obſerved the want of them in ſome later works of this, as well as of other excellent printers, of the ſame place. But allowing them to be in the Terence, and Zarot the inventor, it confutes the date of our Oxford book, as effectually, as if they were of later origin at Venice; as I had reaſon to imagine, from the teſtimony of all the books that I have hitherto met with.

What farther confirms my opinion is, that from the time of the pretended date of this book, anno 1468, we have no other fruit or production from the preſs at Oxford for eleven years next following; and it cannot be imagined that a preſs, eſtabliſhed with ſo much pains and expence, could be ſuffered to be ſo long idle and uſeleſs [R]: whereas, if my conjecture be admitted,

ſand. It is therefore not at all ſurprizing (if true) that the ſignatures, though invented by our Oxford Printer, might not immediately come into general uſe. And conſequently, this particular carries with it no ſuch certain or effectual confutation as our Diſſertator boaſts of." B. & N.

[R] To this it may be anſwered, in the words of Oxo-NIDES : " 1ſt, That his books may have been loſt. Our firſt printers, in thoſe days of ignorance, met with but ſmall encouragement: they printed but few books, and but few copies of thoſe books. In after-times, when the ſame books were re-printed more correctly, thoſe firſt editions, which

admitted, all the difficulties that feem infuperable and inconfiftent with the fuppofed æra of Printing there, will vanifh at once. For allowing the book to have been printed ten years later, anno 1478; then the ufe of fignatures can be no objection: a foreign printer might import them; Caxton take them up from him; and the courfe of Printing and fequel of books publifhed from Oxford will proceed regularly:

Expoficio Sancti Jeronimi in Simbolum Apofto-
  lorum. MCCCCLXXVIII.   Oxonie, 1478
Leonardi Aretini in Ariftot. Ethic. Comment. ib. 1479
Ægidius de Roma, &c. de peccato originali, ib. 1479

which were not as yet become curiofities, were put to common ufes. This is the reafon that we have fo few remains of our firft printers. We have only four books of Theodorick Rood, who feems by his own verfes to have been a very celebrated Printer. Of John Lettou, William de Machlinia, and the School-mafter of St. Alban's, we have fcarce any remains. If this be confidered, it will not appear impoffible that our Printer fhould have followed his bufinefs from 1468 to 1479, and yet Time have deftroyed his intermediate works. But, 2dly, we may account ftill another way for this diftance of time, without altering the date. The Civil Wars broke out in 1469: this might probably oblige our Oxford Printer to fhut up his prefs; both himfelf and his Reader might be otherwife engaged. If this were the cafe, he might not return to his work again till 1479; and the next year, not meeting with that encouragement he deferved, he might remove to fome other country with his types." N.

                                                                Guido

Guido de Columna de Hiftoria Trojana, per
  T. R.   ib. 1480
Alexandri ab Hales, &c. expoficio fuper 3
  Librum de Animâ, per me Theod. Rood. ib. 1481
Franc. Aretini Oratoris Phalaridis Epiftolarum
  e Græco in Latinum Verfio. Hoc opufcu-
  lum in Alma Univerfitate Oxoniæ, a natali
  Chriftiano ducentefima & nonagefima feptima
  Olympiade feliciter impreffum eft. That is, 1485

    " Hoc teodoricus Rood quem Collonia mifit
    Sanguine Germanus nobile p̄ffit ¹ opus.
    Atque fibi focius Thomas fuit Anglicus Huntê
    Dii dent ut Venetos exuperare queant!
    Quam Jenfon Venetos docuit Vir Gallicus artem
    Ingenio didicit terra Britanna fuo.
    Celatos Veneti nobis tranfmittere libros
    Cedite, nos aliis vendimus. O Veneti
    Que fuerat vobis ars primum nota Latini
    Eft eadem nobis ipfa reperta pres ².
    Quamvis fêctos ³ toto canit orbe Britannos
    Virgilius placz ⁴ his lingua Latina tamen [S]."

¹ preffit   ² premens   ³ fejunctos   ⁴ placet

                                         Thefe

[S] The only copy of this book, that I have heard of, is
in the poffeffion of the rev. Mr. Randolph of Deal; and the
firft notice of it was communicated by the rev. Mr. Lewis
of Mergate; who, having been informed that I had drawn
up this little Differtation, very kindly offered me the ufe of
his notes and papers, that he had collected with great pains,
                                             on

Thefe are all the books printed at Oxford before the year 1500, that we have hitherto any certain notice of. I have fet down the colophon and verfes of the laft, becaufe they have fomething curious and hiftorical in them. I had feen one inftance before of the date of a book computed by OLYMPIADS; *Aufonii Epigrammatum libri,* &c.; printed at Venice, anno 1472, with this defignation of the year at the end; " A nativitate Chrifti ducentéfimæ nonagefimæ quintæ Olympiadis anno 11 ;" (Maittaire, Annal. Typ. p. 98, not. [h]) where the printer, as in the prefent cafe, follows the common miftake, both of the ancients and moderns, of taking the OLYMPIAD for a term of FIVE YEARS compleat; whereas it really included but FOUR, and was celebrated every FIFTH; as the LUSTRUM likewife of the Romans [T]. In our Oxford

on *the Hiftory and Progrefs of Englifh Printing to the End of Queen Elifabeth's Reign.* From the perufal of which, though I found no reafon to make any alteration of moment in the prefent Treatife, yet I had a pleafure to obferve a perfect agreement between us, in the chief points on which my argument turns, and to find my own opinion confirmed by the judgment of fo able an antiquary.

Dr. MIDDLETON.

[T] An *Olympiad* was undoubtedly the fpace of FOUR years compleat, and a *Luftrum* of FIVE. But many of the moderns have confounded them, by including each within *four* years. Selden, De Jure Nat. & Gentium, l. iii. p. 360, ed. 1725, obferves the fame; but takes notice that the mif-

take

Oxford book the year of the Olympiad is not diftinguifhed, as in that of Venice, fo that it might
poffibly
take was common to both terms, each of them being fometimes reckoned as FOUR YEARS, fometimes as FIVE :
" Perfimilem in luftris & olympiadibus, quibus nunc *quin-
quennia*, nunc *quadriennia* tribuuntur, fupputandi rationem
nemo nefcit."

Noris takes notice that Ovid *confounds* the fpace of the
Olympiad with the *Luftrum*, Trift. IV. x. 95. " Ovidius,
fcribens fe anno ætatis quinquagefimo exacto, in exilium
deportatum, ait,
" Poftque meos ortus Pifæâ vinctus olivâ
Abftulerat decies præmia victor eques ;"
ubi Pifæorum quadriennes Olympiades cum Romanis Luftris
confundit." Cenotaph. Pifan. p. 2. ed. 1681.

On the other hand, a *Luftrum* is fuppofed to contain only
FOUR years by H. Glareanus in Chronologia Dion.
Halicarn. p. 759, ed. Sylburg. and by Erafmus Schmidius
in his Prolegomena ad Pindarum, p. 15 : " Et ab hoc annorum quatuor completorum circuitu etiam τετραετηρὶς no-
minabatur, plane ut apud Romanos LUSTRUM, quod et
ipfum erat *quatuor* annorum completorum fpatium, ubi *quarto*
quoque exacto anno populus Romanus luftrabatur."

The *Luftrum* is fuppofed to have contained only *four* years
in Pliny N. H. ii. 47 : " Et eft principium Luftri ejus femper
intercalari anno Caniculæ ortu." But he applies the word
in a borrowed fenfe, to exprefs not only the periodical re-
turns, but the cleanfing office of the winds, in that refpect
like the *Luftrum*.

But the proper fenfe of thefe words among the ancients was, that an *Olympiad* fignified FOUR years, and

F a *Luf-*

poſſibly be printed ſomewhat earlier and nearer to the reſt in order of time: but as the ſeventh verſe ſeems to refer

a *Luſtrum* FIVE. The firſt is proved by demonſtrable authority, becauſe the Grecians inſerted their intercalary month of XLV days after three years of 354 days; and appointed theſe games *on the fourth year*, for the regular notoriety of the fact. Blondel, Rom. Cal. liv. II. c. 4; and Prid. Connect. part I. book v. p. 222. ed. Fol.

There are other authorities without number : Ὀλυμπιὰς πληρῦται κατὰ τέτλαρας χρόνυς, Diod. Sic. 44. A. ed. Rhodom.; and no one ever read of above the *fourth* year of the I, II, III, IV, or any other Olympiad. But this period of an OLYMPIAD Dr. MIDDLETON allows.

That the LUSTRUM contained *five* years, is clear, I think, from undoubted teſtimony : in vain elſe would Horace have told the girl ſhe need not ſhun him, as being too rampant, ſince he was arrived at the *eighth* Luſtrum, which ſurely is more probably at XL years of age than XXXII :

"Fuge ſuſpicari,
Cujus OCTAVUM trepidavit ætas
Claudere LUSTRUM." Lib. II. Od. iv. 22.
So again, from Auguſtus's conqueſt of Alexandria, U. C. 724, to his victory over the Rhœti, U. C. 739 (as Dio relates, lib. LIV.), Horace deſcribes

"Fortuna LUSTRO proſpera TERTIO
Belli ſecundos reddidit exitus." Lib. IV. Od. xiv. 37.
Where Acron indeed ſuppoſes the LUSTRUM to be a term of only FOUR years, reckoning XII years from Auguſtus's firſt conſulſhip to the end of the civil wars; in which he is followed, as we obſerved before, by Glareanus.—But, whichſoever it is, *proſe writers* are expreſs for FIVE years. Varro ſays, "Luſtrum nominatum tempus *quinquennale* à luendo,

i. e.

refer to the ftatute 1 Richard III, prohibiting the
Italians from importing and felling their wares in
England

i. e. folvendo, quod *quinto* quoque *anno* vectigalia et tributa
per cenfores folvebantur."—See likewife Horace, l. IV.
Od. i. ver. 6.

It muft be owned Antonius Nebriffenfis, in his Quinqua-
gena, c. xx. printed in the Critici Sacri, tom. IX. ed. Amft.
labours to prove a *Luftrum* to be only FOUR years, from two
or three paffages in the Roman poets, who fometimes take
the liberty of fo applying it; but with much better authority
is it fixed to be FIVE years by Jo. Caftellio, in his Variæ
Lectiones, c. xix. See Fax Artium, tom. IV. c. 19.

Dr. Middleton refumes this fubject in his *Roman Senate,*
A. D. 1747, part I. p. 107, 8vo. [vol. III. p. 429, of the 4to
edition of his works]; and fays, that "as the cenfus was
fuppofed to be celebrated every *fifth* year; and as it was
accompanied always by a *Luftration* of the people; fo the
word *Luftrum* has *conftantly been taken, both by ancients and
moderns,* for a term of FIVE years. Yet we fhall find no
good ground for fixing fo precife a fignification to it; but,
on the contrary, that the Cenfus and Luftrum were, for
the moft part, held irregularly and uncertainly, at very
different and various intervals of time, as the particular exigencies of the ftate required."—But, 1. We have feen it was
" NOT conftantly taken for a term of FIVE years both by ancients and moderns;" fo that this fenfe of FOUR years is
not SOLELY Dr. MIDDLETON's, though he will fuffer no
one elfe to fhare in the honour of it. 2. If it was *conftantly*
taken fo both by *ancients* and *moderns,* one would think that
fhould determine the period; though the Romans might,
for particular exigencies of ftate, vary from the prefcribed

time

England by retail, &c. excepting books written or
printed; which act paffed in 1483, fo it could not be
printed before that year. The third verfe refcues
from oblivion the name of an Englifh printer, THO-
MAS HUNTE, not mentioned before by any of our
Englifh writers, nor difcovered in any other book.
But what I take for the moft remarkable, and lay
the greateft ftrefs upon, is that in the fixth verfe,
" the art and ufe of Printing is affirmed to have
been firft fet on foot and practifed in this ifland by
our own countrymen [U]:" which muft confequently
have

time of the ceremony. 3. Mr. Hooke has fhewn (Obfervations, in Anfwer to L'Abbé Vertot, &c. p. 153, 157),
" that there is good reafon to believe, the feven firft Luftrums, after the eftablifhment of the commonwealth, were
regularly held every *five* years : confequently that there
was fufficient ground in FACT for fixing the term of FIVE
years to the word *Luftrum*.—For the firft SEVEN Luftrums,
under the confuls, will carry us through an interval of exactly
thirty-five years, from A. U. 245."—The Doctor had no
occafion to have laboured this point here at leaft; but his
plenary knowledge in the Roman conftitution would not
fuffer him to bear any contradiction in it. B.

[U] We fhall make no apology for introducing one more
remark from OXONIDES : " Dr. Middleton's tranflation of
the fixth verfe is a fenfe, I believe, ROOD never thought of.
His verfes feem rather defigned to extol *his own prefs* than
that of Caxton ; and the meaning I take to be no more
than this, that the Art of Printing, for which the Venetians, and particularly Jenfon, had been fo famous, was
now

have a reference to Caxton; who has no rival of this country to difpute the honour with him. And fo we are furnifhed at laft from Oxford itfelf, with a teftimony that overthrows the date of their own book.

Theodoric Rood, we fee, came from Cologn (where Caxton had refided many years, and inftructed him-felf in the Art of Printing) in 1471: and, being fo well acquainted with the place, and particularly the printers of it, might probably be the inftrument of bringing over this or any other printer a year or two before (if there really was any fuch) to be

now practifed with equal fuccefs in England. Our Differ-tator's quotation from Caxton will prove but little, unlefs he can fhew, that no printer, at any place, ever talked of the *novelty* of his art, without being the firft importer of it. As to his citations from other later writers, who men-tion Caxton as our firft printer, it may be fufficient to anfwer in his own words, that " it is very unfafe to truft to common hiftory, and neceffary to recur to original tefti-monies, if we would know the ftate of facts with exactnefs." Our ingenious author has himfelf detected feveral miftakes, which our writers have univerfally fallen into, and taken up from each other. If we confider that our Oxford Printer met with very fmall encouragement, printed probably but few books, and did not put his name to thofe, it is no wonder that his name and memory fhould be foon loft; nor will it be furprizing that Caxton fhould run away with the credit of being the firft printer here, who lived many years in great repute, printed a very confiderable number of books, and flourifhed in the funfhine of the court !" N.

employed

employed at Oxford; and the obfcure tradition of
this fact give rife to the FICTION of the RECORD. But
however this be, it feems pretty clear that Caxton's
being fo well known at Cologn, and his fetting up a
prefs at home immediately after his return from that
place, which could hardly be a fecret to Rood, muft
be the ground of the compliment paid to our country,
and the very thing referred to in the verfes [X].

[X] The whole fcope of the above colophon fhews that
the words of the fixth verfe are not to be taken in too
literal a fenfe: " Jenfius, a Frenchman, taught the art
of Printing to the Venetians: but Britain learnt it from
her own ingenuity." Neither of thefe circumftances is
ftrictly true. Jenfon, who began printing at Venice
A. D. MCCCCLXX, was preceded *two* years by Joannes de
Spira; who fays himfelf, in the edition of Cicero's Epiftles
ad Familiares, MCCCCLXIX, that " he firft taught it to the
Venetians:" though the book above referred to, p. 23,
note [N], may feem to difpute his claim. Whether Caxton
or Corfellis brought Printing into Britain, the art was learnt
abroad. The fenfe then of the poet feems to be, that as
Jenfon, a foreigner, had brought Printing to great perfection
at Venice, the Englifh were indebted to a native for fimilar improvements. To denote this excellence, he calls
the impreffion of Thomas Hunte *celatos libros*, books EN-
GRAVED; ufing that term to fet his Printing in an advantageous light, who, with his partner Rood, would in time
excell the Venetians. A like compliment is paid by Nicolas Gupalitinus to Clemens Patavinus, in the preface
to an edition of Mefuas, *De Medicinis univerfalibus*, Ven.
MCCCCLXXI. See MEERMAN, vol. II. p. 35, 36. B. & N.

We

We have one book more, without the name of printer or place, which, from the comparifon of the types with thofe of Rood, is judged to be of his printing, and added to the catalogue of his works by Mr. Lewis in his Mf. Papers, viz.

" Expoficio ac moralifacio tertij capituli trenorum Iheremie prophete. Fol. mccccLXXXII."

And at the end of the index,

" Explicit tabula fuper opus trenorum compilatum per Johann. Latteburij ordinis minorum."

But the identity of the letter in different books, though a probable argument, is not always a certain one for the identity of the prefs.

Befides this early Printing at Oxford, *our Library* gives us proof of the ufe of it likewife, about the fame time, in the city of London, much earlier than our writers had imagined, with the names of two of *the firft printers* there, that none of them take notice of; JOHN LETTOU and WILL. DE MACHLINIA. Of the firft, we have, " Jacobus de Valencia in Pfalterium, &c. excuf. in civitate Londonienfi, ad expenfas Johannem Wilcock, per me Johannem Lettou MCCCCLXXXI. fol." Of the fecond; " Speculum Chriftiani, &c." and at the end; " Ifte libellus impreffus eft in opulentiffima Civitate Londoniarum per Willelmum Machlinia, ad inftanciam necnon expenfas Henrici Urankerbergh mercatoris." Quarto: without date, but in a very coarfe and Gothic character, more rude than Caxton's : and from both thefe printers in partnerfhip, we have the firft edition

tion of the famous *Littleton's Tenures*; printed at London, in a fmall folio, without date; which his Great Commentator, the Lord Chief Juftice Coke, had not feen or heard of: for in the Preface to his Inftitutes, he fays, " That this work was not pub- lifhed in print either by Judge Littleton himfelf, or Richard his fon; and that the firft edition, that he had feen, was printed at Roan in Normandy, ad inftan- ciam Richardi Pynfon, printer to King Henry VIII." We have this edition alfo in our Library, but it is undoubtedly later by thirty or forty years than the other we are fpeaking of; which, as far as we may collect from the time noted above, in which Joh. Lettou printed, was probably publifhed, or at leaft put to the prefs, by the author himfelf, who died in 1481.

Whilft Printing was thus going forward at Weft- minfter, Oxford, and London, there was a prefs alfo employed at St. Alban's, by the *Schoolmafter* of that place; whofe name has not had the fortune to be tranfmitted to us, though he is mentioned as a man of merit, and friend of Caxton. He had drawn up and printed in Englifh, a Book of Chronicles, com- monly called " Fructus Temporum, anno 1483," which I have never been able to meet with: but in a later edition of it after his death, there is the fol- lowing Colophon :

" Here endyth this prefent cronycle of Englond with the frute of tymes, compiled in a booke and enprynted by one fometyme Scolemayfter of St. Albons,

bons, on whoos foule God have mercy, and newly
enprynted at Weftmeftre by Wynkyn de Worde.
MCCCCLXXXXVII."

It was the fame fchoolmafter, without doubt, who
printed three years before in Latin:

" Rhetorica nova Fratris Laurentij Gulielmi de
Soana ordinis minorum, compilata in alma Univerfi-
tate Cantabrigiæ ann. 1478, impreffa apud Villam
Sti Albani. MCCCCLXXX."

This was once in bifhop More's library, being
defcribed in the printed catalogue of his other rare
books [Y]: but it is now loft, or ftolen from that
noble collection; which, by an example of munificence fcarce to be paralleled, was given to our Univerfity by his Majefty King George I, and will remain a perpetual monument of the great mind and
publick fpirit of that Prince.

The fame book is mentioned by Mr. Strype among
thofe given by archbifhop Parker to Corpus-Chrifti
college in Cambridge ; but the words, *compilata in
Univerfitate Cantabrigiæ*, have drawn this learned Antiquary into the miftake of imagining, that it was
printed alfo that year at *our* Univerfity, and of doing
us the honour of remarking upon it, " So ancient
was Printing in Cambridge." Life of Archbifhop
Parker, p. 519.

We have one piece however in our library from
this prefs, in a fmall folio, and at the end of it the
following advertifement :

[Y] Catal. Libror. Manufcriptor. Angl. Oxon. p. 391.

G   ' There

" There in thys boke afore ar contenyt the bokys
of haukyng and huntyng with other plefuris dyverfe.
And alfo of coote armuris a nobull werke. And
here now endyth the boke of blafyng of armys,
tranflatyt and complyt togedyr at Saynt Albons
MCCCCLXXXVI."

After the firft treatife of hawking and hunting,
&c. is added, " Explicit Dam Julyans Barnes in her
boke of huntyng." Though her name be fubjoined
to the firft part only, yet the whole is conftantly
afcribed to her, and paffes for her work. She was
of a noble family, fifter to Richard lord Berners of
Effex, and priorefs of Sopwell nunnery near St.
Alban s : fhe lived about the year 1460, and is celebrated by Leland and other writers for her uncommon learning and accomplifhments, under the name
of Juliana Berners.

I fhall now return to Mr. CAXTON, and ftate as
briefly as I can the pofitive evidence that remains of
his being the firft printer of this kingdom ; for what
I have already alledged, is chiefly negative or circum-
ftantial. And here, as I hinted at fetting out, all our
writers before the Reftoration, who mention the introduction of the art amongft us, give him the credit
of it, without any contradiction or variation. Stowe,
in his Survey of London, fpeaking of the 37th year
of Henry VI, or 1458, fays, " The noble Science
of Printing was about this time found at Magunce by
Joh. Guttemberg, a knight; and WILLIAM CAXTON
of London, mercer, brought it into England, about
the

the year 1471, and firſt practiſed the ſame in the abbey of Weſtminſter." Truſſel gives the ſame account in the Hiſtory of Henry VI, and Sir Richard Baker in his Chronicle: and Mr. Howell, in his Londinopolis, deſcribes the place where the Abbot of Weſtminſter ſet up the firſt preſs for Caxton's uſe, in the Almonry or Ambry. But above all, the famous Joh. Leland, Library-keeper to Henry VIII, who by way of honour had the title of *The Antiquary*, and lived near to Caxton's own time, expreſsly calls him, " The firſt Printer of England," (De Script. Brit. p. 480,) and ſpeaks honourably of his works: and as he had ſpent ſome time in Oxford, after having firſt ſtudied and taken a degree at Cambridge, he could hardly be ignorant of the Origin and Hiſtory of Printing in that Univerſity [Z]. I cannot forbear

[Z] Leland calls Caxton, *The firſt Printer of England*; meaning that he was the firſt who practiſed that art with *fuſile Types*, and conſequently firſt brought it to perfection; and this is not inconſiſtent with Corſellis's having printed earlier at Oxford with *ſeparate cut Types in Wood*, which was the only method he had learnt at Harleim. In like manner the epitaph on THEODORIC MARTENS, who practiſed this art at Aloſt above ſixty years, and died May 28, 1534, aged more than eighty, deſcribes HIM as the *Inventor* of Printing : " Qui artem characterizandi è Superiori Germania, Galliaque, in Inferiorem hanc Germaniam tranſtulit;" that is, *on metal types*, which were univerſally uſed in Germany and Gaul when Martens was a young man, and were ſtyled, by way of eminence, *ars impreſſoria*, or *characteri zandi*. See MEERMAN, vol. I. p. 97, 98. vol. II. p. 34. B. & N.

G 2   adding,

adding, for the fake of a name fo celebrated, the
more modern teftimony of Mr. Henry Wharton,
(Append. ad Cave, Hift. Liter, p. 49;) who affirms
" Caxton to have been the firft that imported the Art
of Printing into this kingdom," On whofe authority, I imagine, the no lefs celebrated M. du Pin ftyles
him likewife the firft printer of England. (Ecclef.
Hift. Cent. xiv. p. 71. ed. Engl.)

To the atteftation of our hiftorians, who are clear
in favour of Caxton, and quite filent concerning an
earlier prefs at Oxford, the works of Caxton himfelf
add great confirmation: the *rudenefs of the letter* ;
irregularity of the page ; *want of fignatures* ; *initial
letters*, &c. in his firft impreffions, give a prejudice
at fight of their being the firft productions of the
art amongft us. But, befides thefe circumftances, I
have taken notice of a paffage in one of his books,
(Recule, &c. in the end of the third book,) that
amounts in a manner to a direct teftimony of it.
" Thus end I this book, &c. and for as moche as in
wrytyng of the fame my penne is worn, myn hande
wery, and myn eyen dimmed with overmoche lokyng
on the whit paper—and that age crepeth on me
dayly—and alfo becaufe I have promyfid to dyverce
gentilmen and to my frendes to addreffe to hem as
haftely as I might this fayd book: Therefore I have
practyfed, and lerned at my grete charge and difpenfe
to ordeyne this fayd book in prynte after the maner
and forme as ye may here fee, and is not wreton with
ponne and ynke as other bokes ben to thende that
                                                    every

every man may have them attones, for all the bookes
of this ſtorye, named, the Recule of the hiſtoryes of
Troyes, thus empryntid as ye here ſee, were begonne
in oon day and alſo finiſhed in oon day, &c." Now
this is the very *ſtyle and language of the firſt Printers,*
as every body knows, who has been at all conver-
ſant with old books. Fauſt and Scheffer, the inventors, ſet the example in their firſt works from Mentz;
by advertiſing the publick at the end of each, " That
they were not drawn or written by a pen (as all
books had been before), but made by a new art and
invention of printing, or ſtamping them by charaċters
or types of metal ſet in forms." In imitation of
whom, the ſucceeding printers, in moſt cities of Europe, where the art was new, generally gave the like
advertiſement; as we may ſee from Venice, Rome,
Naples, Verona, Baſil, Augſburg, Louvain, &c.
juſt as our Caxton, in the inſtance above.

In Pliny's Natural Hiſtory, printed at Venice, we
have the following verſes :

" Quem modo tam rarum cupiens vix lećtor haberet;
 Quiq; etiam fraċtus pœne legendus eram :
Reſtituit Venetis me nuper Spira Johannes ;
 Exſcripſitq; libros ære notante meos.
Feſſa manus quondam, moneo, calamuſq; quieſcat :
 Namq; labor ſtudio ceſſit & ingenio. MCCCCLXVIIII."

In a Spaniſh hiſtory of Rodericus Santius, printed
at Rome :

" De mandato R. P. D. Roderici Epiſcopi Palen-
tini Auċtoris hujus libri, ego UDALRICUS GALLUS
ſine calamo aut pennis eund. librum impreſſi."

At

At the end of Cicero's Philippic Orations :

" Anfer Tarpeii cuftos Jovis, unde, quod alis
  Conftreperes, Gallus decidit ; Ultor adeft
  ULDRICUS GALLUS : ne quem pofcantur in ufum,
  Edocuit pennis nil opus effe tuis,
Imprimit ille die, quantum non fcribitur anno.
Ingenio, haud noceas, omnia vincit homo."

In Eufebius's Chronicon, printed in Latin at Milan :

" Omnibus ut pateant, tabulis impreffit ahenis
  Utile Lavania gente Philippus opus.
Haftenus hoc toto rarum fuit orbe volumen,
  Quod vix, qui ferret tædia, fcriptor erat.
Nunc ope Lavaniæ numerofa volumina noftri
  Ære perexiguo qualibet urbe legunt."

And as this is a ftrong proof of his being *our firft
Printer*; fo it is a probable one, that this very book
was *the Firft* of his printing. I have never feen the
Liber Feftialis, a book without date, which Mr.
Palmer (Hift. of Printing, p. 340), takes for *his firft* :
but the reafons affigned for it, feem to agree full as
well to the Recule of the Hiftories of Troy : and
had he met with this perfeft in the end of the third
book, he would probably have been of another
mind. Caxton had finifhed the tranflation of the two
firft books at Cologn in 1471 : and having then
good leifure, refolved to tranflate the third at the
fame place, (Recule, &c. end of the fecond book ;)
in the end of which, we have the paffage recited
         above.

above. Now in his other books tranflated, as this was, from the French, he commonly marks the pre-cife time of his entering on the tranflation ; of his finifhing it ; and of his putting it afterwards into the prefs : which ufed to follow each other with little or no intermiffion, and were generally compleated within the compafs of a few months. So that in the prefent cafe, after he had finifhed the tranflation, which muft be in, or foon after, the year 1471, it is not likely that he would delay the impreffion longer than was neceffary for the preparing of his materials ; efpecially as he was engaged by promife to his friends, who feem to have been preffing and in hafte, to deliver copies of it to them as foon as poffible.

But as in the cafe of the *Firft Printer*, fo in this of his *Firft Work*, we have a teftimony alfo from him-felf in favour of this book : for I have obferved that, in the recital of his works, he mentions it the firft in order, before "the Book of Cheffe," which feems to be a good argument of its being actually *the firft*. " Whan I had—accomplifhed dyvers werkys and hyftorys tranflated out of frenfhe into englifhe at the requefte of certayn lordes ladyes and gentylmen, as the Recuyel of the Hiftoryes of Troye, the Book of Cheffe, the Hiftorye of Jafon, the Hiftorye of the Mirrour of the World — I have fubmyfed myfelf to tranflate into englifhe the Legende of Sayntes, called Legenda Aurea in latyn—and Wy-lyam Erle of Arondel defyred me—and promyfed to take a refonable quantyte of them—fente to me a
worfhipful

worſhipful gentylman—promyſmg that my ſayd lord
ſhould duryng my lyf geve and graunt to me a yerely
fee, that is to note, a buck in ſommer and a doo in
wynter, &c." (Maittaire, Supplem. ad Tom. I. Annal.
p. 440, not. 4.)

All this, added to the common marks of earlier
antiquity, which are more obſervable in this, than
in any other of his books that I have yet ſeen, viz:
the rudeneſs of the letter; the *incorrectneſs of the language*; and the *greater mixture of French words,* than
in his later pieces; makes me conclude it to be his
firſt work; executed when he came freſh from a long
reſidence in foreign parts. Nay, there are ſome circumſtances to make us believe, that it was actually
printed abroad at Cologn, where he finiſhed the
tranſlation, and where he had been *practiſing and
learning the Art*: for after the account given above,
of his having learnt to print, he immediately adds,
" Whiche book I have preſented to my ſayd re-
doubtid lady Margrete, Ducheſſe of Burgoyne, &c.
and ſhe hath well acceptid hit, and largely rewarded
me, &c." which ſeems to imply his continuance
abroad till after the impreſſion, as well as the tranſlation of the book [AA]. The conjecture is much
ſtrengthened by another fact atteſted of him: That
he did really print at Cologn the firſt edition of
" Bartholomæus de proprietatibus rerum," in Latin:

[AA] It is not ſaid, or ſuppoſed, that Caxton came over
with Corſellis, though he was an aſſiſtant with Turnour in
getting him off. See above, p. 4. B.

which

which is affirmed by Wynkyn de Worde, in an Englifh edition of the fame book, in the following lines [BB]:

" And alfo of your charyte beare in remembraunce
 The foule of William Caxton firft printer of this
 boke,
In laten tongue at Colcyn himfelf to advaunce,
 That every well difpofyd man may thereon loke."

I have never feen, or met with any one who has feen, this *Latin* edition of Bartholomæus by Caxton. It is certain, that the fame book was printed at Cologn by Jo. Koelholf, and the firft that appears of his printing, in the year 1470 [CC], whilft Caxton was at the place, and bufying himfelf in the art: and if we fuppofe him to have been the encourager and promoter of the work, or to have furnifhed the expence of it, he might poffibly on that account be confidered at home as the author of it.

It is now time to make an end, left I be cenfured for fpending too much pains on an argument fo inconfiderable ; where my only view is to fet right

[BB] Maittaire, Ann. Append. ad Tom. I. p. 31.

[CC] Ibid. p. 296.—This fuppofition is entirely overthrown by an undoubted proof of the date MCCCCLXX, in the copy Dr. MIDDLETON refers to, having been altered from MCCCCLXXXIII, by an erafure. See Note [L], p. 21. It is however extremely probable, from the verfes of Wynkin de Worde, that the *firft edition* of this book was printed by Caxton at Cologn, without the name of place or printer. See MEERMAN, vol. I. p. 59, 60. N.

fome little points of hiftory, that had been falfely or negligently treated by our writers, to which the courfe of my ftudies and employment engaged me to pay fome attention : and above all, to do a piece of juftice to the memory of our worthy countryman WILLIAM CAXTON ; nor fuffer him to be robbed of the glory fo clearly due to him, of having *firft imported into this kingdom* an art of great ufe and benefit to mankind : a kind of merit, that, in the fenfe of all nations, gives the beft title to true praife, and the beft claim to be commemorated with honour to pofterity : and it ought to be infcribed on his monument, what I find declared of another printer, Bartholomæus Bottonus of Reggio ; PRIMUS EGO IN PATRIA MODO CHARTAS ÆRE SIGNAVI, ET NOVUS BIBLIOPOLA FUI, &c. (Maittaire, Append. ad tom. I. p. 432. in not.)

He had been bred very reputably in the way of trade, and ferved an apprenticefhip to one Robert Large, a mercer ; who, after having been fheriff and lord mayor of London, died in the year 1441, and left by will, as may be feen in the Prerogative-office, XXIIII marks to his apprentice WILLIAM CAXTON : a confiderable legacy in thofe days, and an early teftimonial of his good character and integrity.

From the time of his mafter's death, he fpent the following thirty years beyond fea, in the bufinefs of merchandize : where, in the year 1464, we find him employed by Edward IV, in a publick and honourable negotiation, jointly with one Richard Whitehill, efq; to tranfact and conclude a treaty of commerce
between

between the king and his brother-in-law the Duke of
Burgundy, to whom Flanders belonged. The com-
miffion ftyles them, " Ambaffiatores, Procuratores,
Nuncios, & Deputatos fpeciales;" and gives to both
or either of them full powers to treat, &c. [DD].

Whoever turns over his printed works, muft contract a refpect for him, and be convinced that he preferved the fame character through life, of an honeft,
modeft man; greatly induftrious to do good to his
country, to the beft of his abilities, by fpreading
among the people fuch books as he thought ufeful to
religion and good-manners, which were chiefly tranflated from the French. The novelty and ufefulnefs
of his art recommended him to the fpecial notice and
favour of the great; under whofe protection, and at
whofe expence, the greateft part of his works were
publifhed. Some of them are addreffed to king Edward the Fourth; his brother the Duke of Clarence;
and their fifter the Dutchefs of Burgundy; in whofe
fervice and pay he lived many years, before he began
to print; as he oft acknowledges with great gratitude. He printed likewife for the ufe, and by the
exprefs order, of Henry the Seventh; his fon Prince
Arthur; and many of the principal nobility and
gentry of that age: all which confirms the notion of
his being *the Firft Printer*; for he would hardly
have been fo much careffed and employed, had there
been an earlier and abler artift all the while at Ox-

[DD] Rymer, Fœd. tom. XI. p. 536. Item Maittaire,
Ann. Typ. Append. ad tom. I. p. 33.

ford,

ford, who yet had no employment at all for the space of eleven years.

It has been generally afferted and believed, that all his books were printed in the Abbey of Weftminfter; yet we have no affurance of it from himfelf, nor any mention of the place before the year 1477 : fo that he had been printing feveral years, without telling us where. There is one miftake however, worth the correcting, that the writers have univerfally fallen into, and taken up from each other ; That John Iflip was the abbot who firft encouraged the art, and entertained the artift in his houfe : whereas I find upon enquiry, that he was not made abbot till four years after Caxton's death ; and that Thomas Milling was abbot in 1470, made bifhop of Hereford a few years after [1474], and probably held the abbey *in commendam* till the year 1485, in which John Eftney next fucceeded : fo that Milling, who was reputed a great fcholar, muft have been the generous friend and patron of Caxton, who gave that liberal reception to an art fo beneficial to learning [EE].

This fhews how unfafe it is to truft to common hiftory, and how neceffary it is to recur to original teftimonies, where we would know the ftate of facts with exactnefs. Mr. EACHARD, at the end of Edward the Fourth's reign, among the learned of that age, mentions WILLIAM CAXTON as a writer of Englifh Hiftory ; but feems to doubt whether he was the fame with the printer of that name. Had he ever

[EE] Willis's Hiftory of Mitred Abbeys, vol. I. p. 206.

looked

looked into Caxton's books, the doubt had been
cleared; or had he confulted his Chronicle of England [FF], which it is ftrange that an Englifh Hiftorian could neglect, he would have learnt at leaft to
fix the beginning of that reign with more exactnefs,
as it is noted above, juft TWO YEARS earlier than he
has placed it in his Hiftory of England [GG].

There

[FF] With deference to the opinion of CAXTON, it is
placing his authority too high, when moft, if not all, our
Englifh Chronicles are made to fubmit to his, and a new
æra is prefcribed to one of our kings by it. It is needlefs
to appeal to contemporary hiftorians, where we are capable
of producing demonftration. We have already vindicated
the true reading of our old Almanacks, and exterminated a
falfe one from CAXTON's Chronicle. But the Doctor raifes
a triumph on his great difcovery; and poor Eachard is
fingled out to be lafhed, for not reading this Chronicle, or
not making the fame ufe of it as the Doctor does. See
above, Note [D], p. 8. B. & N.

[GG] *Juft ONE year*, Dr. MIDDLETON fhould have faid;
EACHARD fixing it very right, 4 March, 1461, *according
to the common computation in thofe days*, (i. e. 1460-1); the
Doctor 1459, *according to our computation*, (i. e. 1459-60).
But this Gentleman feems refolved to be at variance with
that Hiftorian as far as poffible. He gives us his doubts;
but fo much the worft fide of them, that it is but juft to let
the Hiftorian fpeak for himfelf: " In this reign flourifhed
JOHN HARDING and WILLIAM CAXTON, both writers of
the Englifh Hiftory. And that which now began to give
encouragement to Learning, was the famous Art of Printing,
which was firft found out in Germany by JOHN GUTTEN-
BERGHEN

There is no clear account left of Caxton's age: but he was certainly very old, and probably above fourfcore, at the time of his death. In the year 1471 he complained, as we have feen, of the infirmities of age creeping upon him, and feebling his body; yet he lived twenty-three years after, and purfued his bufinefs, with extraordinary diligence, in the abbey of Weftminfter, till the year 1494 [HH], in which he died; not in the year following, as all, who write of him, affirm. This appears from fome verfes at the end of a book, called, " Hilton's Scale of Perfection," printed in the fame year:

" Infynite laud with thankynges many folde
    I yelde to God me focouryng with his grace
This boke to finyfhe which that ye beholde
    Scale of Perfeccion calde in every place
Whereof th'auctor Walter Hilton was
    And Wynkyn de Worde this hath fett in print
In William Caxftons hows fo fyll the cafe,
    God reft his foule. In joy ther mot it ftynt.
           Inpreffus anno falutis MCCCCLXXXXiiii."

BERGHEN about 1440, or fomewhat later, and was brought into England by WILLIAM CAXTON, a mercer of LONDON, and PROBABLY the fame with the Hiftorian, who firft practifed the fame in the Abbey of Weftminfter 1461, and the 11th of this reign." The Hiftorian writes fo agreeably to the Doctor's hypothefis, that one would think he need not be fo much afhamed of his company. B. & N.

[HH] No longer than the year 1491, as Mr. Ames has fince proved from his epitaph, and the edition of Catal. Biblioth. Harl. vol. III. p. 127. B.

3

Though

Though he had printed for the ufe of Edward IV, and Henry VII; yet I find no ground for the notion which Palmer takes up, that the firft printers, 'and particularly CAXTON, were fworn fervants and printers to the crown : for Caxton, as far as I have obferved, gives not the leaft hint of any fuch chara&er or title; though it feems to have been inftituted not long after his death: for of his two principal workmen, Richard Pynfon and Wynkin de Worde, the one was made Printer to the King; the other, to the King's mother the Lady Margaret. Pynfon gives himfelf the firft title, in " The Imitation of the Life of Chrift," printed by him at the commandment of the Lady Margaret, who had tranflated the fourth book of it from the French, in the year 1504: and Wynkin de Worde affumes the fecond, in " The feven Penitential Pfalms," expounded by bifhop Fifher, and printed in the year 1509.

But there is the title of a book given by Palmer, that feems to contradi& what is here faid of Pynfon : viz. " Pfalterium ex mandato vi&oriofiffimi Angliæ Regis Henrici Septimi, per Gulielmum Fanque, Impifforem Regium, anno MDIIII;" which being the only work that has ever been found of this printer, makes it probable, that he died in the very year of its impreffion, and was fucceeded immediately by Richard Pynfon : whofe ufe of the fame title fo foon after, fhews the writers to be miftaken in this, and feveral other particulars relating to his hiftory, as well as that of Wynkin de Worde, which it is not my prefent bufinefs to explain.

Mr.

Mr. MEERMAN's ACCOUNT

OF THE

ORIGIN OF PRINTING.

WITH

REMARKS.

IT may feem fomewhat ftrange that the original of Printing has hitherto eluded all the refearches of the learned; and that this art, which has given light to all others, fhould itfelf remain in obfcurity. And yet the wonder will ceafe, if we confider that it was invented as a more expeditious method of multiplying books than by writing, and was at firft defigned to counterfeit it; confequently was concealed for private intereft, rather than revealed to the proprietor's honour and the public advantage. As Mr. MEERMAN has endeavoured to reconcile fome difficulties on this head in Latin, we fhall briefly lay them before the Englifh Reader, by which he will fee the many miftakes of every one of our lateft writers on the fubject; and that the difficulties have arifen, not fo much from the want of hiftorical evidences, as from not attending to the true fenfe of them; from overlooking it in its

imperfect

imperfeƈt ſtate, and as an embryo not born into day-
light.

The three cities, Mr. MEERMAN obſerves, which
have the faireſt claim to this honour, are Harleim,
Mentz, and Straſburgh : to each it is to be aſcribed
in a qualified ſenſe ; the improvements the one made
upon the other entitling them all, in ſome ſort, to the
merit of the invention.

The firſt teſtimony of the inventor is that recorded
by Hadrian Junius, in his Batavia, p. 253, ed. Lugd.
Bat. 1588 ; which, though it has been rejeƈted by
many, is of undoubted authority. Junius had the
relation from two reputable men, Nicolaus Galius [A],
who was his ſchoolmaſter, and from Quirinius Tale-
ſius, his intimate and correſpondent. He aſcribes it
to Laurentius the ſon of John (Ædituus, or Cuſtos, of
the cathedral at Harleim, at that time a reſpeƈtable
office), upon the teſtimony of Cornelius, ſometime
a ſervant to Laurentius, and afterwards bookbinder

[A] Galius ſeems to be the ſame who is called *Claes Lot-
tynſz. Gael,* Scabinus Harlemi, as it is in the Faſti of that
city, in the years 1531, 1533, and 1535. Quirinius in
the ſame Faſti is called *Mr. Quiryn Dirkſzoon.* He was many
years amanuenſis to the great ERASMUS, as appears from his
Epiſtle, 23 July, 1529, tom. III. Oper. p. 1222. He was
afterwards Scabinus in 1537 & ſeq. ; and conſul in 1552
& ſeq. But in the troubles of Holland he was cruelly killed
by the Spaniſh ſoldiers, 23 May, 1573. There are ſome
Letters of HADRIAN JUNIUS to this TALESIUS, in the
Epiſtolæ Junianæ, p. 198.

to the cathedral, an office which had before been
performed by Francifcan fryars. His narrative was
thus : " That walking in a wood near the city. (as the
" citizens of opulence ufe to do) he began at firft to
" cut fome letters upon the rind of a beach tree;
" which, for fancy's fake, being impreffed on paper,
" he printed one or two lines, as a fpecimen for his
" grandchildren (the fons of his daughter) to fol-
" low. This having happily fucceeded, he medi-
" tated greater things (as he was a man of ingenuity
" and judgement); and firft of all, with his fon-in-law
" THOMAS-PETER (who by the way left three fons,
" who all attained the confular dignity), invented a
" more glutinous writing ink, becaufe he found the
" common ink funk and. fpread; and then formed
" whole pages of wood, with letters cut upon them;
" of which fort I have feen fome effays, in an ano-
" nymous work, printed only on one fide, intituled,
" *Speculum noftræ falutis*; in which it is remarkable,
" that in the infancy of Printing (as nothing is com-
" plete at its firft invention) the back fides of the pages
" were pafted together, that they might not by their
" nakednefs betray their deformity. Thefe beachen
" letters he afterwards changed for leaden ones, and
" thefe again for a mixture of tin and lead [*ftanneas*],
" as a lefs flexible and more folid and durable fub-
" ftance. Of the remains of which types, when they
" were turned to wafte metal, thofe old wine-pots
" were caft, that are ftill preferved in the family-
" houfe, which looks into the market-place, inhabited
                                        " afterwards

" afterwards by his great grandfon GERARD THOMAS,
" a gentleman of reputation, whom I mention for the
" honour of the family, and who died old a few years
" fince. A new invention never fails to engage curio-
" fity. And when a commodity never before feen ex-
" cited purchafers, to the advantage of the inventor,
" the admiration of the art increafed, dependents were
" enlarged, and workmen multiplied, the firft ca-
" lamitous incident. Among thefe was one JOHN,
" whether, as we fufpect, he had ominoufly the name
" of FAUSTUS [B], unfaithful and unlucky to his
" mafter, or whether it was really a perfon of that
" name, I fhall not much inquire; being unwilling to
" moleft

[B] Etymology, which leads to the true meaning of
words, is a kind of hiftorical knowledge, which renders the
ftudy of Grammar more pleafing. To produce the various
lights which it affords, would be endlefs; but we may be
indulged in mentioning one inftance, which is immediately
connected both with our profeffion and the perfon here
mentioned. JOHN FAUST, or FUST, is by many fuppofed to
have derived his name from *Fauflus*, happy ; and Dr. *Fauflus*
feems to carry an air of grandeur in the appellation : but very
erroneoufly. *John Faufl*, or *Fufl*, is no more than *John
Hand*, whence our name *Fift*. This is of fmall moment in
itfelf, if an eminent German Critic (ERASMUS SCHMIDIUS)
had not refined too much upon it, and led himfelf into a
miftake by his too great knowledge. The famous editions
of Tully's Offices by JOHN FUST (for there are certainly
two, one in 1465, the other in 1466) have uniformly, at
the end, the following co.ophon. The firft of them,

Prefens

" moleft the filent fhades, who fuffer from a confciouf-
" nefs of their paft actions in this life.   This man,
" bound

Prefens Marci tulii clariffũ opus. Johannes fuft Mogũtinus civis. nõ atramẽ-
to. plumali cãna neq̧ acrea. Sed arte qua-
dam perpulcra. *Petri manu pueri mei* feliciter effeci finitum.   anno M.cccc.lxv.

The fecond is worded with more exactnefs, and ftands thus :
Prefens tulii M. clariffũ opus Jo-
hannes fuft Mogũtinus civis. nõ attramẽ-
to. plumali cãna neq acrea. Sed arte qua-
dam perpulcra. *manu Petri de Gernfheim pueri mei* feliciter effeci finitum. anno M.cccc.lxvi. *quarta die
menfis februarii.* τc.

Now Schmidius, in Nov. Teft. Norimbergæ, 1658, p. 5,
tells us he was poffeffed of a copy of this book, with the firft
of thefe colophons; and had heard of, but never feen, the
other. This learned Critic, full of the meaning of the name
Fuft, fays : " Moneo non recte fcribi *manu Petri,* &c. quafi
το *manu* effet ablativus inftrumenti ; quum ab autore, licet
σολοίκως, ufurpetur in genitivo, *arte Petri Manu,* & fit
proprium, 𝕻𝖊𝖙𝖊𝖗 𝕱𝖚𝖘𝖙 𝖔𝖉𝖊𝖗 𝕱𝖆𝖚𝖘𝖙, non appellativum."
The Latin indeed, if fo read, is not difagreeable to the rudenefs of the age, when that language, though much diffufed,
was yet read and written with a very low degree of accuracy.
But the misfortune is, Schmidius's reading is inconfiftent
with hiftory : for it does not appear that JOHN FUST had any
fon or fervant named PETER, except PETER SCHOEFFER de
Gernfheim, to whom, for being an ufeful affiftant to him in
his art, he gave his daughter CHRISTIAN (or DINAH) FUST in
marriage ;

" bound by oath to keep the fecret of Printing, when
" he thought he had learnt the art of joining the
" letters,

marriage ; and it is not clear that it was a cuftom in Germany for the hufband to change his name for the wife's.—
There can be very little doubt, therefore, of there having
been *two editions*, unlefs the variation is accounted for by
fuppofing that the colophon in Schmidius's copy was printed
off before it was fully corrected ; which might poffibly be the
cafe, becaufe the month and day feem to have been omitted;
at leaft, Schmidius, who is very particular here, has not
copied them, though they are ufually added in the colophons
of that age.   But, after all, if Schmidius had *feen*, in the colophon of 1466, *manu* PETRI DE GERNSHEIM *pueri mei*, he
muft have given up his interpretation of *manu.*—We leave
this however as a curiofity to be fought after ; and as highly
to be prized, when poffeffed, as Duke Lauderdale's Bible,
with the forgery in it of, *Paul, a* KNAVE *of Jefus Chrift**.

Mr. Maittaire (in his Annales Typographicæ, 1719, vol. I.
p. 60.) tells us, " he has COMPARED the editions of 1465
and 1466 ; and finds them, except the variation of the
colophon, EXACTLY the fame."—Mr. Palmer, in 1732,
either not knowing this circumftance, or not attending to
it, fays (Hift. of Printing, p. 81), " It is very probable
" thefe editions may be *the fame*, the laft fheet only re-
" printed ; *which may be eafily known by comparing them to-*
" *gether* ; and it were to be wifhed, that fome of the cu-
" riofo's of Oxford would take that trouble, fince they are
" both there, as appears from Ant. Wood's lift."—The
reverend Dr. Taylor, chancellor of Lincoln, afterwards

* See an account of this book in the Notes of Fortefcue Aland,
Efq; on Lord Chief Juftice Fortefcue on Abfolute and Limited
Monarchy, p. 42.

examined

" letters, the method of cafting the types, and other
" things of that nature, taking the moſt convenient
" time

examined both editions, and favoured us with the following remark : " I HAVE COMPARED THEM too, and
" EXACTLY ; and find them VERY DIFFERENT : every
" page indeed beginning and ending alike, but not every
" line : the ſhape alſo of ſeveral letters being very different,
" particularly *m*, as thus, ꝏ. M.   J. T."

The *s*, *ſ*, and *d*, are likewiſe differently formed in theſe copies. See Catal. Bibl. Harleian. vol. IV. A. D. 1744, p. 520.

Theſe editions are taken notice of in the *Bibliographie
Inſtructive des Belles Lettres, par Guillaume François de Bure,
le Jeune*, p. 151. The firſt of them has ſo many variations
as to induce that writer to think there were *three* or *four*
editions in 1465.

	One edition has,		The other,
In the Title of the volume,	*A*rpínatís	——	*a*rpmatís
In the Preface,	Prefaſío	——	Prefacío
	*in*cípit	——	*m*cípit
	nic*h*íl	——	ni*h*íl
In the Latin verſes at the end of Book III.	cupí*en*s	——	cupíſs
At the end of the Paradoxes,	ſu*n*t	——	ſū̃t, and a line added in red.
In the Verſus XII Sapientum,	ſapientu͂	——	ſapientū
Les *Ecuſſons* de Schoyffer,		——	(wanting.)

In the firſt edition of 1465, before the ode of Horace,
Diffugere nives, &c. printed at the end, is this inſcription,
in two lines :

Manlio Torquato Flaccus, de vite hu-
mane brevitate. per comparationem tēpis, hec ;

The titles of *Three Precepts of Friendſhip* are tranſpoſed in
the firſt edition, and right in the ſecond ; and many other
variations, too minute to mention.

Mr.

" time that was poffible, on Chriftmas eve, when all
" were cuftomarily employed in luftral facrifices,
" feizes the collection of types, and all the imple-
" ments his mafter had got together, and, with one
" accomplice, marches off to Amfterdam, thence to
" Cologn, and at laft fettled at Mentz, as at an
" afylum of fecurity, where he might go to work
" with the tools he had ftolen. It is certain that
" in a year's time, viz. in 1442, the *Doctrinale* of
" Alexander Gallus, which was a Grammar much
" ufed at that time, together with the *Tracts* of Peter
" of Spain, came forth there, from the fame types as
" Laurentius had made ufe of at Harleim."

Thus far the narrative of Junius, which he had frequently heard from Nicolaus Galius; to whom it was related by Cornelius himfelf, who lived to a great age, and ufed to burft into tears upon reflecting on the lofs his mafter had fuftained, not only in his fubftance, but in his honour, by the roguery of this fervant, his former affociate and bedfellow. Cornelius, as appears by the regifters of Harleim cathedral, died either in 1515 or the beginning of the

Mr. De Bure adds, that in *(Clement's* or) the *third* edition the *Four Lines of Title* are wanting; which may have been omitted in *that copy* by miftake, as thofe lines are *in red* in the other copies; and therefore this is moft probably not a different edition.

He fuppofes alfo a *fourth* edition in *vellum*; but that is no criterion. A copy in vellum of the edition in 1466 is in the B.itifh Mufeum. B. & N.

following

following year; fo that he might very well give this information to Nicolaus Galius, who was fchool-mafter to Hadrian Junius.

Though this circumftance is probable as to the main fact, yet we muft fet afide the evidence of it in fome particulars. The firft obvious difficulty is noticed by Scriverius; " that the types are faid to be made of the *rind* of beach, which could not be ftrong enough to bear the impreffion of the prefs." This is removed, if, inftead of the *bark*, we fubfti-tute a *bough* of the beach. The idea of the *bark*, when Junius wrote this, was perhaps ftrong in his mind, from what Virgil tells us (Ecl. v. 13.) of its being ufual to cut words on the *bark* of a beach ; and thence he was eafily led to make a wrong application of it here.

2. The letters were at firft *wooden*, and are faid to be afterwards exchanged for *metal* types; from which the wine-pots were formed, remaining in the time of Junius. According to tradition, Printing was carried on in the fame houfe long after the time of Laurentius : thofe pots might therefore be formed from the wafte metal of the printing-houfe, after the ufe of *fufile types* became univerfal. But Laurentius feems to have carried the art no farther than *feparate wooden types*. What is a remarkable confirmation of this, HENRY SPIEGHEL, who wrote in the fixteenth century, in a poem intituled *Hertfpiegel*, fays thus [in Dutch] : " Thou firft, Laurentius, to fupply the defect " of wooden tablets, adaptedft *wooden types*, and
                                    " afterwards

" afterwards didſt connect them with a thread, to imi-
" tate writing. A treacherous ſervant procured to
" himſelf the honour of the diſcovery. But Truth
" itſelf, though deſtitute of common and wide-ſpread
" fame ; Truth, I ſay, ſtill remains." No mention
in the Poem of *metal types* ; which had he been
robbed of, as well as the wooden ones, would ſcarcely
have been paſſed over in ſilence.

When LAURENTIUS firſt deviſed his rough ſpecimen
of the art, can only be gueſſed at. He died in 1440,
after having publiſhed the *Speculum Belgicum*, and
two editions of *Donatus*, all of different *wooden types* ;
which it is probable (conſidering the difficulties he
had to encounter, and the many artiſts whom he
muſt neceſſarily have had occaſion to conſult) coſt him
ſome years to execute ; ſo that the firſt eſſay might
be about 1430, which nearly agrees with PETRUS
SCRIVERIUS, who ſays, the invention was about ten
or twelve years before 1440 [C].

3. What

[C] Scriverius's account is ſomewhat different from that
of Junius. He tells us, that "Laurentius, walking in the
" wood, picked up a ſmall bough of a beech, or rather of
" an oak tree, blown off by the wind; and, after amuſing
" himſelf with cutting ſome letters on it, wrapped it up
" in paper, and afterwards lay down to ſleep. When he
" awaked, he perceived that the paper, by a ſhower of rain or
" ſome accident, having got moiſt, had received an impreſſion
" from theſe letters; which induced him to purſue the ac-
" cidental diſcovery." Scriverius however proceeds, according to Mr. Meerman, on a wrong hypotheſis; as he

K takes

3. What was the specimen which he first diverted himself with in cutting, after three centuries, one would think impossible to be discovered. And yet JOH. ENSCHEDIUS, a printer, thinks he was so happy as to find it, being an old parchment *Horarium*, printed on both sides, in eight pages, containing the Letters of the Alphabet, the Lord's Prayer, the Apostles Creed, and three short prayers. And Mr. MEER-MAN having shewn this to proper artists, who were judges of these matters, they gave it as their opinion that it agreed exactly with the description of Junius. It is conformable to the first edition of the Dutch *Speculum Salvationis*, and the fragments of both *Donatus's* of Holland, which are both the works of the same Laurentius, and were preceded by this. In these types, which are certainly moveable, cut, and uneven, there is a rudeness which Mr. MEERMAN has not observed in any other instance. There are no numbers to the pages, no signatures, no *direction words* [D],

no

takes it for granted that the first essays were on *wooden blocks*, and not on *separate* wooden types.—Junius's account is from the servants of Laurentius; Scriverius's is grounded on imagination, and on an error of Scaliger. The former is clear; the latter, when the circumstance of *going to sleep* is considered, seems to border on the marvellous. N.

[D] It is a ridiculous conceit of some, that these were called *custodes* from Laurentius's name *Coster*; whereas they undoubtedly received their name from their office, as being *keepers* to the pages, that they may follow in order; and were *never used* by Laurentius or his family. See MEER-

no divifions at the end of the lines; on the contrary, a fyllable divided in the middle is feen, thus, *Sp iritu* in p. 8. l. 2, 3. There are no diftinctions nor points, which are feen in the other works of Laurentius; and the letter *i* is not marked with an accent, but with a dot at the top. The lines throughout are uneven. The fhape of the pages not always the fame, not (as they fhould be) rectangular, but fometimes rhomb-like, fometimes an *ifofcele trapezium*; and the performance feems to be left as a fpecimen of his piety and ingenuity in the effay of this new-invented art. Mr. MEERMAN has given an exact engraving of this fingular curiofity.

There are FOUR other credible teftimonies, who lived before Junius, that confirm the relation [E] of

MAN, vol. I. p. 77. For the introduction of *folios* and *fignatures*, fee note [Q], p. 27, 28. To which we may add, that Mr. MEERMAN thinks the firft inftance of either *folios* or *running-titles* was in the "Sermones LEON. de UTINO, "Parifii, 1477;" though the ufe of *folios* is fo obvious, that they are moft probably to be found in old Mff. N.

[E] Coæval almoft with CORNELIUS was ULRIC ZELL, a native of Hanover, the firft who practifed Printing at Cologn, who attained the rudiments of the art by officiating as Corrector of the Prefs under Fuft or Gutenberg, as appears by the *Chronicon* of Cologn, a work written under his own infpection. ZELL being a German, and profeffedly an advocate for the caufe of Mentz, his teftimony in favour of Harleim (where he allows the foundation of the art was laid) will be acknowledged unexceptionable. See MEERMAN, vol. I. p. 60. B. & N.

Cornelius,

Cornelius, and yet feem to derive their authority from a different channel; and who all mention the theft of Laurentius's fervant, and his fetting up at Mentz (fee MEERMAN's *Documenta*, LXXXI—LXXXIV); viz.

1. " Zurenus, in JOANNIS VAN ZUYREN reliquiæ,
" ex opufculo deperdito, cui tit. Zurenus junior, five
" de prima, et inaudita hactenus vulgo, et veriore
" tamen artis typographicæ inventione dialogus, nunc
" primum confcriptus, autore Joan. Zureno, Harlemeo,
" ad ampliffimum virum N. N. affervatæ—a Petr.
" Scriverio in Laurea Laurentiana, c. II."

2. " THEODORUS VOLCKARDI COORNHERTIUS in
" dedicatione præmiffa verfioni Belgicæ Officiorum
" Ciceronis, edit. Harlem. 1561, atque infcripta Con-
" fulibus, Scabinis, et Senatoribus ejufdem urbis."

3. " HENRICUS PANTALEON, Lib. de viris illuftri-
" bus Germaniæ, part. II. p. 397, feq. ed. Bafil. 1565."

4. " LUDOVICUS GÜICCIARDINUS, Defcrizzione di
" tutti i Paefi Baffi, edita Antwerpiæ, typis Gul. Sylvii,
" 1567, p. 180, in defcriptione urbis Harlemi."

But PANTALEON, it fhould be obferved, is miftaken when he afcribes to JOHN FUST the invention of Printing, and more fo when he fays that he took in John Schœffer, inftead of Peter, partner: for John, the fon of Peter, and grandfon of Fauftus by his daughter, was certainly not born in 1440, fince he was famous in 1548 See MARCHAND, Hift. de l'Imprimerie, p. 50. Befides, this writer afferts that Nic. Jenfon followed the art in France; who, though he was

born

born in that kingdom, yet practifed Printing no where but at Venice. He mentions likewife two remarkable circumftances; one, of the manner of hiding the types, when they had ftolen them, " eos literas *in fac-* " *culis claufis* fecum in officinas tuliffe, atque ab- " euntes abftuliffe;" the other, of the honour paid to the firft artifts [F]. The greateft part of what he has written is borrowed from WIMPHELINGIUS, Epit. Rer. German.

But, whatever elfe may appear doubtful in the narrative of Junius, it is very clear that the firft effays of the art are to be attributed to LAUREN-TIUS [G], who ufed only *feparate wooden types.* He died

[F] Mr. MEERMAN obferves, that the following of other manual profeffions was accounted a derogation to nobility; but that this Art conferred honour on its profeffors. Hence it was very early practifed by many who were of noble families, and even by eminent Ecclefiaftics. JOHN GUTENBERG was, in 1465, received *inter Aulicos* by the Elector ADOLPHUS : and the Emperor FREDERICK III. permitted Printers to wear gold and filver; and both *Typographi* and *Typothetæ* were honoured by him with the privilege of wearing coat-armour ; " Typothetis fcil. aquilæ, " typographis autem gryphi, pede altero pilam tinctoriam " unguibus tenentis, fcutum donavit, cum aperta galea, et " fuperimpofita ei corona." MEERMAN, vol. I. p. 47, 48, 207. And fee hereafter, p. 99.

[G] It may not be improper here to give an abridgement of Mr. MEERMAN's account of LAURENTIUS and his family :—He was born at Harleim about 1370, and executed

feveral

died in 1440; and Mr. MEERMAN is of opinion (on the authority of GUICCIARDINI) that the types were ſtolen very ſoon after his death.

Moſt

ſeveral departments of magiſtracy in that city.—Thoſe writers are miſtaken, who aſſign to him the ſurname of COSTER, or aſſert that the office of Ædituus was hereditary in his family. In a diploma of ALBERT of Bavaria, in 1380, in which, among other citizens of Harleim, our Laurentius's *father* is mentioned by the name of " JOANNES " LAURENTII filius," BEROLDUS is called Ædituus, who was ſurely of another family; and in 1396 and 1398 HENRICUS à LUNEN enjoyed that office; after whoſe reſignation, Count ALBERT conferring on the citizens the privilege of *electing* their Ædituus, they, probably ſoon after, fixed on LAURENTIUS; who was afterwards called COSTER, from his office, and not from his family name, as he was deſcended from an illegitimate branch of the *Gens* BREDERODIA. His office was very lucrative; and that he was a man of great property, the elegance of his houſe may teſtify. That he was the *inventor* of Printing, is plain from the narrative of Junius. His firſt work was the *Horarium* abovementioned, p. 66; the next the *Speculum Salutis*, in which he introduced *pictures* on *wooden blocks*; then *Donatus*, the larger ſize; and afterwards the ſame work in a leſs ſize. All theſe were printed on *ſeparate moveable wooden types*, faſtened together by threads. If it be thought improbable that ſo ingenious a man ſhould have proceeded no farther than the invention of *wooden types*; it may be anſwered, that he printed for profit, not for fame; and *wooden* types were not only *at that time* made ſooner and cheaper than *metal* could be, but were ſufficiently durable for the ſmall impreſſions of each book he muſt neceſſarily

have

Moſt writers agree that there was a robbery by
ſome one ; though they differ in the particulars,
and

have printed.—His preſs was nearly ſhaped like the common wine-preſſes.—He printed ſome copies of *all* his books
both on paper and vellum.—It has been very erroneouſly
ſuppoſed that he quitted the profeſſion, and died broken-
hearted : but it is certain that he did not live to ſee the
art brought to perfection.—He died in 1440, aged 70 ; and
was ſucceeded either by his ſon-in-law THOMAS PETER,
who married his only daughter LUCIA ; or by their imme-
diate deſcendants, PETER, ANDREW, and THOMAS; who
were old enough (even if their father was dead, as it is
likely he was) to conduct the buſineſs, the eldeſt being at
leaſt 22 or 23. The loſs they had ſuſtained by the robbery
would be repaired without much difficulty or expence ; and
they ſtill had the aſſiſtance of CORNELIUS, and other ſer-
vants of their grandfather.—What books they printed, it is
not eaſy to determine ; they having, after the example of
LAURENTIUS, (more anxious for profit than for fame) neither added to their books their names, the place where they
were printed, or the date of the year.—Their firſt eſſays
were new editions of *Donatus* and the *Speculum.* They
afterwards re-printed the latter, with a Latin tranſlation ;
in which they uſed their grandfather's wooden pictures ; and
printed the book partly on *wooden blocks,* partly on *wooden
ſeparate types,* as Mr. MEERMAN clearly proves, vol. I.
p. 135 ; who has given an exact engraving of *each ſort,* taken
from different parts of the ſame book, which was publiſhed
between the years 1442 and 1450. Nor did they ſtop here ;
but continued to print ſeveral editions of the *Speculum* both
in Latin and in Dutch. Four editions of this book are yet
to

and even in the name of the perfon who is faid to
have committed it. Thofe who deny the whole ftory
ground their opinion, 1. on the improbability of fuch
a faƈt being done on fo public a night, when the
whole city muft neceffarily have been awake ; 2. on
the great difficulty there muft have been in conveying
a large quantity of materials through the gates of

to be feen. There are many other books in being, certainly printed in Holland, which may with probability be
affigned to this family. Of the following ones in particular, there can be no doubt : " Hiftoriæ ALEXANDRI
" Magni ;" " FLAVII VEDATII [for VEGETII] RENATI
" Epitome de re Militari ;" "Opera varia à THOMAS KEM-
" PIS." Of each of thefe Mr. MEERMAN has given an
engraved fpecimen. They were all printed with *feparate
wooden types* ; and, by their great neatnefs, are a proof that the
defcendants of LAURENTIUS were induftrious in improving
his invention. And hence an additional argument may be
brought in favour of CORSELLIS, whofe impreffions were
likewife on *feparate wooden types*, are remarkable for their
neatnefs, and much refembling thofe of Harleim, whence
he came to Oxford about 1459. See above, p. 7, 8.—
KEMPIS was printed at Harleim in 1472, and was the laft
known work of LAURENTIUS's defcendants, who foon after
difpofed of all their materials, and probably quitted the employment; as the ufe of *fufile types* was about that time
univerfally diffufed through Holland by the fettling of
MARTENS at Aloft, where he purfued the art with reputation for upwards of fixty years. PETER and ANDREW, the
two eldeft grandfons of LAURENTIUS, perifhed in the civil
war of 1492. See MEERMAN's *Index primus*. B. & N.

Harleim,

Harleim, which no one was permitted to pafs at night unexamined, or through the feveral other towns in the way to Mentz; and, 3. on his having been permitted to exercife the art after his arrival in that city, without being molefted by any judicial complaint from thofe whom he had robbed.

To this it may be anfwered, that JUNIUS wrote in a very figurative manner; and, to exprefs his abhorrence of the crime in the ftrongeft light, accufed the robber of having ftolen " the collection of types, and " ALL the inftruments his mafter had got together." But furely much lefs would effectually have anfwered the purpofe of this unfaithful fervant. Skilled as he muft have been in every department of the bufinefs, it could be no difficulty to him to get proper workmen, in any country, who could (by his inftructions) fupply him with a prefs, and every thing elfe that was bulky. All that he really wanted was, *a fmall quantity of wooden types,* as a pattern to cut others from. Thefe he might pack up in a fmall parcel, either late at night, or early in the morning; which it would be an eafy matter to conceal till the city gates were opened. And indeed no time could be more fuitable to fuch a purpofe than that which is affigned to it; fince, no bufinefs being performed either on that or the following day, he would be far out of their reach when the lofs fhould be difcovered; and it is highly probable that (CORNELIUS and the other fervants of the family being employed in their religious duties) he had an oppor-

L   tunity

tunity of being fome hours alone in the houfe, and of plundering unmolefted whatever he had occafion for. Perhaps he even obtained permiffion from the family of his deceafed mafter to take a journey to Amfterdam or Mentz, for which fome plaufible pretence might readily be formed. However this was, it would be eafy to prevent the difcovery of his fraud till he fhould be fafe out of the territories of Holland. It was his bufinefs therefore to take the fhorteft route (through Amfterdam and Cologn) to Mentz, his native city. Here he fixed his refidence, and had little to apprehend from the tribunal of Harleim, whofe fentence (if any fuit was even entered againft him) could extend no farther than to banifh him from a country which he never more intended to re-vifit.

Having fhewn that a theft was actually committed, it will be neceffary to inquire who was the guilty perfon. It is clear from all accounts that his name was JOHN [H]. ZURENUS exprefsly calls him *a foreigner*; and there is little doubt of his being a native of Mentz : why elfe fhould he have chofen to fettle in that city, at a diftance from his family

[H] It is fomewhat fingular, that many of the earlieft Printers were thus named; as, GEINSFLEICH fenior and junior, FUST, MEIDENBACHIUS, and PETERSHEMIUS; a circumftance which induced the Leipfic Printers to confecrate St. JOHN the Baptift's anniverfary to feftivity, as is obferved by Jo. STORIUS, in a Differtation preferved by WOLFIUS, Monum. Typogr. tom. II. p. 475, *in not.* N.

2

and

and friends, whofe affiftance he would need in fo new and arduous an undertaking? What his furname was, is an interefting inquiry. JUNIUS, after fome hefitation, afcribes it to JOHN FUST; but with injuftice: for he was a wealthy man, who affifted the firft printers with money at Mentz; and though he afterwards was proprietor of a printing-office, yet he never, as far as appears, did any part of the bufinefs with his own hands; and confequently he could never have been a fervant to LAURENTIUS. Nor is the conjecture of SCRIVERIUS better founded, who fixes it upon JOHN GUTENBERG, who (as appears by authentic teftimonies) refided at Strafburg from 1436 to 1444, and during all that period employed much fruitlefs labour and expence in endeavouring to attain this art. Mr. MEERMAN once thought, " it " might poffibly be either JOHN MEIDENBACHIUS " (who, we are told by SEB. MUNSTER and the au- " thor of *Chronographia Moguntinenfis*, was an af- " fiftant to the firft Mentz printers); or JOHN PETER- " SHEIMIUS (who was fometime a fervant to FUST " and SCHOEFFER, and fet up a printing-houfe at " Francfort 1459); or, laftly, fome other perfon, " who, being unable through poverty to carry on " the bufinefs, difcovered it to GEINSFLEICH at " Mentz." But more authentic intelligence afterwards convinced him there were two perfons of this name, who appear to have been brothers, and that the junior was diftinguifhed by the additional appellation of GUTENBERG. Thefe were both printers;

L 2 and

and their hiftory fhall be given in as fhort a compafs
as poffible [I].

All things being fully confidered, it appears that
JOHN GEINSFLEICH fenior was the difhoneft fervant,
who was born at Mentz, and who, in the papers
publifhed by KOHLERUS, we find there in the year
1441, and not before: for though he was of a good
family, yet was he poor, and feems to have been
obliged, as well as his brother, to have fought his
livelihood in a foreign country; and perhaps was

[I] There were two JOHN GEINSFLE:CHES of Mentz,
the fenior called GEINSFLEICH κατ᾽ ἐξοχήν; the other diftinguifhed by the name of GUTENBERG. They were both
poor; though of a family diftinguifhed by knighthood,
They were both married men, and were moft probably
brothers, as it was not une mmon in that age for two brothers to have the fame Chriftian name. Thefe both appear in a difreputable light. The eldeft robbed his mafter,
with many aggravating circumftances. The youngeft was
remarkably contentious; and, after entering into a contract
of marriage with ANNA, a noble girl of *The Iron Gate*, re-
fufed to marry her till compelled by a judicial decree; and
afterwards cared not what became of the lady, but left her
behind at Strasburgh when he removed to Mentz. He had
not only frequent quarrels with his wife; but with AN-
DREW DRIZFHEN, ANDREW HEILMANN, and JOHN
RIFF, all of whom were affociated with him at Strasburg,
in his different employments, of making of looking-glaffes,
polifhing of precious ftones, and endeavouring to attain the
art of Printing: and with thefe he involved himfelf in three
law-fuits. See MEERMAN, vol. I. p. 163, &c.   N.

content

content to be under LAURENTIUS, that when he had
learnt the art, he might follow it in his own. But, to
leave conjecture, we may produce some certain testimonies.

1. It is what JUNIUS himself says, that the person
who stole the types did it with a view to set up elsewhere; nor is it likely that he would either make no
use of an art he had seen so profitable to LAUREN-
TIUS, or that he would teach it to another, and sub-
mit to be again a servant.

2. The Lambeth Record, which is printed above,
p. 3, from Mr. ATKYNS, tells us, that " Mentz gained
" the art by the brother of one of the workmen of
" Harleim, who learnt it at home of his brother,
" who after set up for himself at Mentz."—By the
strictest examination of the best authorities, it is plain
that by these *two brothers* the two GEINSFLEICHES
must be meant. But as the younger (who was called
GUTENBERG) was never a servant to LAURENTIUS,
it must be the senior who carried off the types, and
instructed his brother in the art; who first applied
himself to the business at Strasburg, and afterwards
joined his elder brother, who had in the mean time
settled at Mentz.

What is still stronger, two Chronologers of Strafburgh, the one named DAN. SPEKLINUS, the other
anonymous (in MEERMAN's *Documenta*, N° LXXXV,
LXXXVI) tell us expressly, that JOHN GEINSFLEICH
(viz. the senior, whom they distinguish from GUTEN-
BERG), having learnt the art by being servant to its

first

firſt inventor, carried it by theft into Mentz, his native country. They are right in the fact, though miſtaken in the application of it; for they make *Straſburg* the place of the invention, and MENTELIUS the inventor, from whom the types were ſtolen : but this is plainly an error; for GEINSFLEICH lived at Mentz in 1441, as appears from undoubted teſtimonies; and could not be a ſervant to MENTELIUS, to whom the forementioned writers aſcribe the invention in 1440, though more antient ones do not attempt to prove that he began to print before 1444 or 1447. Nor will the narrative agree better with GUTENBERG, who was an earlier printer than MENTELIUS, ſince, among the evidences produced by him in his law ſuit, 1439, no GEINSFLEICH ſenior appears, nor any other ſervant but LAURENTIUS BEILDEK. The narration therefore of the theft of GEINSFLEICH, being ſpread by various reports through the world, and ſubſiſting in the time of theſe Chronologers, was applied by them (to ſerve the cauſe they wrote for) to Strasburg; but ſerves to confirm the truth, ſince no writer derives the printing ſpoils from any other country than Holland or Alſatia. The Chronologers have likewiſe, inſtead of FUST, called GUTENBERG the wealthy man; who, from all circumſtances, appears to have been poor; they alſo call SCHOEFFER the ſon-in-law of MENTELIUS, when it is clear that he married the daughter of FUST.

Printing being introduced from Harleim into Mentz, GEINSFLEICH ſenior ſet with all diligence to carry

it

it on; and publifhed in 1442 ALEXANDRI GALLI *Doctrinale* [K], and PETRI HISPANI *Tractatus*; two works, which, being fmall, beft fuited his circum-ftances, and for which, being much ufed in the fchools, he might reafonably expect a profitable fale. This has been difputed by many writers, becaufe none of thefe editions have been found. But they undoubtedly were publifhed, though without the name of place or printer; as the preceding books at Harleim were printed, and the following ones at Mentz till the year 1457; and therefore, if any at prefent remain in the collections of the curious, they are only difcoverable to fuch as are well acquainted with the types of LAURENTIUS. Nay, it is poffible that the copies may be all torn and deftroyed, having been ufed only by fchoolboys, as hath happened to

[K] ERASMUS teftifies that thefe tracts were received in fchools, when he was a young man, *Ep. ad* HENR. BOUIL-LUM, 31 Aug. 1513, Opp. tom. III. p. 103. Of this Grammar of ALEXANDER DE VILLA DEI, written in verfe, fee among others Jo. ALB. FABRICIUS, *Biblioth. Lat. med. et infim. Latinit.* lib. I. and Jo. LEICHIUS in *Supplem.* MAITTAIRII, at the end of *Orig. Typogr. Lipf.* p. 119. *feq.* Of PETER OF SPAIN, who flourifhed in the clofe of the XIIIth century, fee NICH. ANTONIUS's *Biblioth. Hifpan. vet.* lib. VIII. c. 5. p. 52; and of his *Parva Logicalia,* or *Thefaurus Sophifmatum,* which JUNIUS here points out, Sir THOMAS MORE's *Apology for the Folly of* ERASMUS deferves to be read, tom. III. Opp. ERASMI, p. 1897, & feq. See MEERMAN, vol. I. p. 94. B.

both

both the Harleim editions of DONATUS; or the remainder of them were fuppreffed by the Mentz printers, whofe improvement in the art had rendered
thefe books ufelefs; or, if any of them are ftill remaining, they are hidden in obfcurity, as many others
of the firft effays of printing; fome of which Mr.
MEERMAN difcovered, which none have before mentioned [L]; and more, it is hoped, will be brought to
light

[L] In proof of this affertion, Mr. MEERMAN particu-
lary mentions *two editions* of this *Grammar* of ALEXANDER
DE VILLA DEI, unknown to Mr. MAITTAIRE and otheis.
One, and that in his own library, without time, place, or
printer, beginning with the work itfelf, *Scribere clericulis paro
doctrinale novellis*, was publifhed in quarto in the Roman
character, and that *cut*, as appears from the inequality of
the type, and contains twenty-eight lines in a page; which
may be reckoned, by all the marks, among the firft editions
printed in Italy, about 1470, or before.

The other, which the celebrated Mr. JACOB BRYANT
fhewed Mr. MEERMAN, is in folio, in the Roman character,
and *cut* too, with fome elegance, thirty lines long, and has
the following remarkable infcription at the end:

" Alexandri de Villa Dei Doctrinale (Deo laudes) fe-
" liciter explicit. Impreffum fat incommode. Cum aliqua-
" rum rerum, quæ ad hanc artem pertinent, impreffori
" copia fieri non potuerit in hujus artis inicio: pefte Ge-
" nuæ, Aft, alibique militante. Emendavit autem hoc
" ipfum opus Venturinus Prior, Grammaticus eximius, ita
" diligentèr, ut cum antea Doctrinale parum emendatum in
" plerifque locis librariorum vitio effe videretur, nunc illius
" cura

will be brought to light, by a comparison with the valuable specimens of early printing, which Mr. MEERMAN's plates exhibit. Nor can any thing material be opposed to JUNIUS's relation, except the silence of JOHN SCHOEFFER of those works, in his narration preserved by TRITHEMIUS. The reason is, he passes over the whole history of *moveable wooden types*, as not worth his notice; and relates only the particulars of *metal types*, first those which had their

" cura et diligentia adhibita in manus hominum quam
" emendatissimum veniat. Imprimentur autem posthac libri
" alterius generis literis, et eleganter arbitror. Nam et
" fabri et aliarum rerum, quarum hactenus promptor in-
" digus fuit, illi nunc Dei munere copia est, qui cuncta
" disponit pro suae voluntatis arbitrio. AMEN."

As VENTURINUS dwelt at Florence, and in 1482 published there *the Rudiments of the Latin Grammar*, it is probable this *Doctrinale* was printed in the same place likewise, and by the same artists, who afterwards printed the works of VIRGIL with SERVIUS's *Commentary* in 1472, viz. BERNARD and DOMINICK CENNINI. For if the inscription subjoined to VIRGIL, and to be seen in MAITTAIRE, tom. I. p. 320, be compared with what is above exhibited, it will be manifest that, to print the Prince of Poets, they had got a workman who could cast the letters (for *cast* they were), as they had hopes of getting, they tell us, in the inscription to the *Doctrinale*. Thus this Grammar, by the CENNINI, is the first book printed at Florence; which Dom, MANNI seems not to have known, in his Dissertation on the first impressions at Florence, lately published in the Italian language. See MEERMAN, vol. I. p. 94, 95. B. & N.

M   faces

faces *cut on caſt bodies* (which Mr. MEERMAN at *firſt*
erroneouſly thought to have been not *caſt* at all, but
cut out of metal, an opinion he correĉts in the con-
cluſion of his work), and afterwards *complete fuſile
types*, both firſt uſed at Mentz.

This twofold invention of Printing is what no one
has obſerved before Mr. MEERMAN; and yet clears
up all the diſputes between Harleim and Mentz:
the firſt with *ſeparate wooden types* at Harleim, by
LAURENTIUS, about 1430, and after continued by
his family; the other with *metal types*, firſt *cut*, and
afterwards *caſt*; which were invented at Mentz, but
not uſed in Holland till brought thither by THEO-
DORIC MARTENS at Aloſt [M].

The

[M] This THEODORIC MARTENS, or the ſon of MAR-
TIN, who is frequently mentioned in ERASMUS's Epiſtles, had
the following epitaph, in German, put up in the church
of the monaſtery of the Wilhelmites at Aloſt : " Here lies
" THEODORIC MARTENS, who brought the art of cha-
" raĉteriſing, from Upper Germany and France, to Lower
" Germany. He died May 28, 1534." By *the art of
characteriſing* is to be underſtood printing with metal types
is undoubted, as we have ſhewn above, p. 43, note [Z].
So that PROSPER MARCHAND is miſerably miſtaken,
when, in his *Lexicon Criticum*, tom. II. p. 29, art. MAR-
TENS, he produces this epitaph as a proof againſt LAU-
RENTIUS's being the firſt printer.—The firſt books yet
known of MARTENS's printing were at Aloſt 1473. See
MARCHAND, *Hiſt. de l'Impr.* p. 63. But he ſeems to
have had ſeveral partners, who came with him into Holland,

The circumftance of there being two brothers of the name of JOHN GEINSFLEICH will lead us to the meaning of the Poet, in thefe verfes, fubjoined to the firft editions of JUSTINIAN's *Inftitutes*, printed by PETER SCHOEFFER in 1468:

" Hos dedit eximios fculpendi in arte magiftros,
　　Cui placet en ma&tos arte fagire viros,
　Quos genuit ambos urbs Moguntina JOHANNES,
　　Librorum infignes protocharagmaticos,
　Cum quibus optatum PETRUS venit ad *Polyandrum,*
　　Curfor pofterior, introëundo prior;
　Quippe quibus præftat fculpendi lege, fagitus
　　A folo dante lumen et ingenium."

By " ambos JOHANNES," all have hitherto thought to be meant FAUSTUS and GUTENBERG, not fufficiently attending to the firft two lines, which fome have left out as needlefs. That FAUSTUS, a man of wealth, practifed Printing with his own hands, or caft the types, no one ever dreamt; nor do even thofe moderns fay he did, who think he is here meant. It will be difficult, therefore, to perfuade us, that SCHOEFFER, in whofe praife, and with whofe con-

---

land, as it is certain Jo. of WESTPHALIA did. See MAITTAIRE, Annal. Typogr. tom. I. p. 334, ed. 2. And fince MATTHAEUS VAN DER GOES appears a printer at Antwerp 1472, who in that year printed *het boeck van Tondalus vifioen* in quarto, THEODORIC confequently returned about that period, from Germany and France, into his own country. See MEERMAN, vol. I. p. 98. B. & N.

fent,

fent, thefe verfes were made, would fuffer FAUSTUS, his father-in-law, to be complimented for his fkill in an art to which he had no pretence.   The truth is, the two JOHNS are no other than GEINSFLEICH fenior and GUTENBERG, who were the firft inventors of *metal types.*   And yet Mr. MEERMAN thinks FUST is not wholly unmentioned, but fufpects he is hinted at by the word *Polyandrum,* to whom both the GEINS-FLEICHES and PETER SCHOEFFER applied as to the commmon patron of all printers, whom he affifted with his bounty and counfel.   He had certainly the furname given him of Gutman or GOODMAN, as Jo. CARION informs us in his *Chronicle,* which name feems to be alluded to by a new fignification of the word *Polyander,* the Alterman, or one who had *many men* under his direction.   *Polyandrum* has been alfo explained by many writers to mean the *penetralia artis,* and fuppofed to allude to CHRIST's fepulchre, which PETER firft entered, though he came to it after JOHN.——SCHELHORNIUS, however, *Amœnit. Liter.* tom. IV. p. 301, fufpected fome *unknown perfon* was here intended [N].

Which of the two brothers invented the *metal types,* hiftory does not inform us.   GEINSFLEICH fenior had printed in 1442 the *Grammar* of ALEXDER DE VILLA DEI, and the *Logicalia* of PETER OF SPAIN on *wooden types;* but, finding them not fuffi-

[N] See MEERMAN, vol. I. p. 176, 177.

3   ciently

ciently durable, foon faw the expediency of ufing
metal. In 1443 he hired the houfe **Zum-jungen,**
and was affifted with money by Fust, who in return had a fhare of the bufinefs; and about the fame
time John Meidenbachius was admitted a partner,
as were fome others, whofe names are not tranfmitted
to our times; and in 1444 they were joined by Gutenberg, who for that purpofe quitted Strasburg. It
feems likely therefore that Geinsfleich fenior firft
thought of ufing *metal types*; but, his eyes failing
him, he inftructed Gutenberg in his art, which
reached no farther than cafting the *fhanks* of the
letters, or little fquare blocks of *metal,* which (Po-
lydore Vergil tells us) was firft thought of in the
1442, the very year in which Geinsfleich publifhed
his firft effays on *wooden types*; which had not anfwered his expectations. But, fince the brothers are
both called *protccharagmatici,* it is fafeft, with Wimphelingius, to look upon both as the inventors of
this improvement.

Whilft the *metal types* were preparing, which muft
have been a work of time, feveral works were printed,
both on *wooden feparate types* and *wooden blocks*;
which were well adapted to fmall books of frequent ufe, fuch as the *Tabula Alphabetica,* the *Catholicon,* Donati *Grammatica,* and the *Confeffionalia.*
Thefe were certainly printed by this partnerfhip, and
alfo fome *wooden pictures.*

From the abovementioned printers, in conjunction,
after many fmaller effays, the *Bible* was publifhed in
1450.

1450, with *large cut metal types* [O]. And it is no wonder, confidering the immenfe labour this work coft, that it fhould be feven or eight years in completing. In this fame year the partnerfhip was diffolved; and a new one entered into, in Auguft, between Fust and Gutenberg; the former fupplying money, the latter fkill, for their common benefit. Various difficultics arifing occafioned a law-fuit for the money which Fust had advanced, which was carried againft Gutenberg. A diffolution of this partnerfhip enfued in 1455; and in 1457 a magnificent edition of the *Pfalter* was publifhed by Fust and Schoeffer, with a remarkable commendation, in which they affumed to themfelves the merit of a new invention (viz. of *metal types*), " adinventionem arti- " ficiofam imprimendi ac characterizandi." This book was uncommonly elegant, and in fome meafure the work of Gutenberg; as it was four years in the prefs, and came out but eighteen months after the partnerfhip was diffolved between him and Fust.

[O] Many writers have fuppofed that this was the edition of which fome copies were fold in France, by Fust, as manufcripts, for the great price of five or fix hundred crowns, which he afterwards lowered to fixty, and at laft to lefs than forty. But it was the fecond and more expenfive edition of 1462, that was thus difpofed of, when Fust went to Paris in 1466, and which had coft 4000 florins before the third quaternion (or quire of four fheets) was printed. See Meerman, vol. I. p. 6. 151, 152. N.

The

The latter continued in poffeffion of the printing-office : and GUTENBERG, by the pecuniary affiftance of CONRAD HUMERY, fyndic of Mentz [P], and others, opened another office in the fame city ; whence appeared, in 1460, without the printer's name, the *Catholicon* Jo. DE JANUA, with a pompous colophon, in praife of its beauty, and afcribing the honour of the invention to the city of Mentz [Q].

It

[P] At the death of GUTENBERG, CONRAD HUMERY took poffeffion of all his printing materials : and engaged to the Archbifhop ADOLPHUS, that he never would fell them to any one but a citizen of Mentz. They were, however, foon difpofed of to NICHOLAS BECHTERMUNTZE, of Altavilla, who, in 1469, publifhed *Vocabularium Latino-Teutonicum*, which was printed with the fame types which had been ufed in the *Catholicon.* This very curious and fcarce *Vocabulary* was fhewn to Mr. MEERMAN, by Mr. BRYANT, in the valuable library at Blenheim, belonging to his Grace the Duke of MARLBOROUGH. It is in quarto, thirty-five lines long, contains many extracts from the *Catholicon*, and is called *Ex quo* from the Preface beginning with thofe words. See MEERMAN, vol. II. p. 96. N.

[Q] This edition, having been publifhed without a name, has been almoft univerfally afcribed to FUST and SCHOEFFER. But Mr. MEERMAN thinks it was not the work of thofe printers; 1. becaufe the whole form of their colophons varies from this, and theirs were always printed with *red* ink, and this with *black*; 2. becaufe it has not *their names* to it, which they never omitted after 1457; and, 3, becaufe the fhape of the letter is very different from any

N that

It was a very handſome book, though inferior to the
Pſalter which had been publiſhed in 1457 by FUST
and SCHOEFFER. Both the *Pſalter* and *Catholicon* were
printed on *cut metal types* [R]. It may not be improper to obſerve here, that as the *Pſalter* is the earlieſt

that they uſed. As there was no other printing-office at
Mentz in 1460 but theirs and GUTENBERG's, Mr. MEER-
MAN confidently aſcribes it to the latter; and accounts very
probably for the omiſſion of the printer's name; 1. by the motive of his publication being *profit*, rather than *fame*; and, 2.
(which was a ſtronger reaſon) left his claim to the invention
ſhould be contradicted by SCHOEFFER, who was then living
in the ſame city. The laſt motive ſeems to have had its
uſe; for SCHOEFFER never took any public notice of it, till
he publiſhed the *Inſtitutiones* JUSTINIANI, in 1468, where
he informs his readers, that the two GEINSFLEICHES,
though very ſkilful men, had not arrived to ſo great perfection in the art as himſelf. See above, p. 83. This was
the firſt edition of the *Catholicon* Jo. DE JANUA; the *Catholicon* which was printed by GEINSFLEICH with *wooden
types* (ſee above, p. 85) being only a *ſmall Vocabulary* for
the uſe of ſchools. The Straſburgh edition, by MENTE-
LIUS, which was publiſhed without a name, was not printed
till long after, probably not before 1469. See MEERMAN,
vol. II. p. 96—99. N.

[R] GUTENBERG never uſed any other than either *wooden*
or *cut metal types* till the year 1462. In 1465 he was made
a counſellor of ſtate by the Elector ADOLPHUS, with an annual penſion; and died in February 1468. His elder brother
GEINSFLEICH died in 1462. Their epitaphs are printed
by Mr. MEERMAN, vol. II. p. 154. 295. N.

book which is known to have a genuine date, it became a common practice, after that publication, for
printers to claim their own performances, by the
addition of their names.

The progress of the art has been thus traced
through its *second* period, the invention of *cut metal
types.* But the honour of *completing* the discovery
is due to PETER SCHOEFFER [S] *de Gernsheim.*

A very clear account of this final completion of
the types is preserved by TRITHEMIUS [T]: "Post
" hæc inventis succefferunt subtiliora, inveneruntque
" modum *fundendi formas* omnium Latini alphabeti

[S] In German, Schoeffer; in Latin, OPILIO; in
English, SHEPHERD.—He is supposed by Mr. MEERMAN
to have been the first ENGRAVER on Copper Plates. The
Poet, whose verses we have cited in p. 84, says of him,
 " Natio quæque suum poterit reperire charagma
 " Secum ; nempe stylo præminet omnigeno."
It is not quite certain, however, as Mr. MEERMAN observes,
whether this is meant for a compliment to his skill in what
is now called ENGRAVING ; it may perhaps mean only that
he was able to *cut types* to represent all languages. See
MEERMAN, vol. I. p. 253. N.

[T] Annales Hirsaugienses, tom. II. ad ann. 1450,
p. 421. As this book was finished in 1514, and TRI-
THEMIUS tells us he had the narrative from SCHOEFFER
himself about thirty years before, this will bring us back
to 1484, when SCHOEFFER must have been advanced in
years, and TRITHEMIUS about twenty-two years old, who
died in 1516. See Voff. Hist. Lat. l. III. c. 10. FABR.
Med. & Infim. Ætat. l. IX. B.

N 2   " literarum,

" literarum [U], quas ipfi *matrices* nominabant ;
" ex quibus rurfum æneos five ftanneos characteres
" fundebant, ad omnem preffuram fufficientes, quos
" prius manibus fculpebant. Et revera ficuti *ante*
" xxx *ferme annos* ex ore Petri Opilionis de Gern-
" fheim, civis Moguntini, qui gener erat primi artis
" inventoris, audivi, magnam a primo inventionis
" fuæ hæc ars imprefforia habuit difficultatem.—
" Petrus autem memoratus Opilio, tunc famulus
" poftea gener, ficut diximus, inventoris primi,
" Johannis Fuft, homo ingeniofus et prudens, faci-

[U] Mr. MEERMAN (vol. II. p. 47.) fuppofes there is an
error in this paffage, and that it fhould be read, " fundendi
" formas omnium Latini alphabeti literarum [EX IIS] quas
" ipfi *matrices* nominabant;" and explains it to mean, "That
" they found out a method *fundendi formas* (that is, of *cafting*
" *the bodies* only) of all the letters of the Latin alphabet, FROM
" WHAT *they called matrices* (on which they *cut the face* of each
" letter) ; and *from the fame kind of matrices* a method was in
" time difcovered of cafting the *complete letters (æneos five*
" *ftanneos characteres)* of fufficient hardnefs for the preffure
" they had to bear, which letters were before (that is, when
" the *bodies only were caft)* cut fingly." But this interpretation
is itfelf *obfcure* ; and, with fubmiffion, the paffage from
TRITHEMIUS needs no correction. The fimple fenfe is,
That a mode was invented of *ftamping the fhape of the letters*
in *matrices*, from which were *caft* the *complete types.*—The
firft operation of the Founder at prefent is, to cut the *face* of
the letter on a *fteel punch*; this he ftrikes into a *copper matrix* ;
and from *matrices* the *metal types* are caft, without any further procefs. N. See hereafter, p. 143.

" liorem

"liorem modum *fundendi characteres* excogitavit, et
"artem, ut nunc eft, complevit."

Another ample teftimony in favour of Schoeffer
is given by Jo. Frid. Faustus of Afchaffenburg,
from papers preferved in his family: "Peter
"Schoeffer of Gernfheim, perceiving his mafter
"Fust's defign, and being himfelf ardently defirous
"to improve the art, found out (by the good pro-
"vidence of God) the method of cutting *(incidendi)*
"the characters in a *matrice*, that the letters might
"each be fingly *caft*, inftead of being *cut*. He pri-
"vately *cut matrices* for the whole alphabet;
"and when he fhewed his mafter the letters caft
"from thefe matrices, Fust was fo pleafed with the
"contrivance, that he promifed Peter to give him
"his only daughter Christina in marriage; a pro-
"mife which he foon after performed. But there
"were as many difficulties at firft with thefe let-
"ters, as there had been before with *wooden* ones;
"the metal being too foft to fupport the force of the
"impreffion : but this defect was foon remedied, by
"mixing the metal with a fubftance which fuffi-
"ciently hardened it." This account has the more
probability in it, as coming from a relation of Fust,
yet afcribing the merit to Schoeffer [X]. It agrees

[X] Meerman, vol. I. p. 183. who copied this teftimony from Wolfius, Monum. Typograph. vol. I.
p. 468. feq.

too with what JOHN SCHOEFFER tells us [Y], "that
"in 1452 FUST completed the art, by the help of
"his fervant PETER SCHOEFFER, whom he adopted
"for his fon, and to whom he gave his daughter
"CHRISTINA [Z] in marriage, *pro digna laborum*
"*multarumque adinventionum remuneratione.* — F U S T
"and SCHOEFFER concealed this new improvment,
"by adminiftering an oath of fecrecy to all whom
"they intrufted, till the year 1462; when, by the
"difperfion of their fervants into different countries,
"at the facking of Mentz by the archbifhop AD-
"OLPHUS, the invention was publicly divulged."

The firft book printed with thefe *improved types*
was DURANDI *Rationale,* in 1459; at which time,
however, they feem to have had only *one fize* of
caft letters, as all the larger charafters in the head-
lines, &c. are printed with *cut* types, as appears

[Y] In a colophon to the *Breviarium* TRITHEMII. See
MEERMAN, vol. II. p. 144.†

[Z] It is fomewhat remarkable that JOHN SCHOEFFER
fhould be miftaken in his mother's *name*; which, however,
Mr. MEERMAN thinks he was, fince his father (in a contraft made, in 1477, with his kinfman FUST, about twenty
copies in vellum, and 180 in paper, of the *Decretals* of
Gregory IX, being the refidue of an impreffion ptinted in
1473) exprefsly calls his wife **Dynen,** i. e. DINAH;
which KÖHLERUS, who has printed this contraft, fuppofes to be a diminutive of CHRISTINA: though DINAH
(or DEBORAH) is a very different name from CHRISTINA.
MEERMAN, vol. I. p. 184. But fee, more particularly,
the Remarks in our Appendix, p. 143. N.

plainly

plainly by an infpection of the book [AA]. From this time to 1466 FUST and SCHOEFFER continued to print a confiderable number of books; particularly the two famous editions of TULLY's *Offices*, which we have given an account of above, p. 59. In their earlieft books, they printed more copies on *vellum* than on *paper*, which was the cafe both of their *Bibles* and TULLY's *Offices*. This, however, was foon inverted; and *paper* introduced for the greateft part of their impreffions, a few only being printed on *vellum*, for curiofities, and for the purpofe of being *illuminated* [BB]. How long FUST lived, is uncertain; but in 1471 we find SCHOEFFER was in partnerfhip with CONRAD HENLIF and a kinfman of his mafter FUST [CC]. He publifhed many books after the death of his father-in-law [DD]; the laft of which that can be difcovered is a third edition of the *Pfalter* in 1490, in which the old *cut* types of the firft edition were ufed [EE].

This Differtation fhall be clofed with a fhort account of the claim of *Strasburgh*. It has been al-

[AA] MEERMAN, vol. II. p. 98.
[BB] Ibid. vo'. I. p. 8.
[CC] Ibid. p. 7.
[DD] SCHWARZIUS, *Primar. Docum. de Orig. Typogr.* par. II. p. 4. has enumerated *forty-eight* books (*omnes grandiori forma*) printed by SCHOEFFER before 1492. And Mr. MEERMAN adds ftill more to that number. See vol. I. p. 253.
[EE] MEERMAN, vol. II. p. 52.

ready mentioned, that GUTENBERG was engaged in
that city in different employments; and, among others,
in an endeavour to attain the art of Printing [FF].
That thefe endeavours were unfuccefsful, is plain
from an authentic judicial decree of the fenate of
Strafburgh, in 1439, after the death of ANDREW
DRIZEHEN [GG].

But there are many other proofs that GUTENBERG
and his partners were never able to bring the art to
perfection.

[FF] See above, p. 76, note [I].

[GG] Their firft attempts were made about 1436, with
wooden types. Mr. MEERMAN is of opinion that GEINS-
FLEICH junior (who was of an enterprizing genius, and
had already engaged in a variety of projects) gained fome
little infight into the bufinefs by vifiting his brother, who
was employed by LAURENTIUS, at Harleim, but not fufficient to enable him to practife it.   It is certain, that, at the
time of the law-fuit, in 1439, much money had been expended, and no profit arifing; and the unfortunate DRIZE-
HEN, in 1438, on his death-bed, lamented to his con-
feffor, that he had been at great expence, without having
been re-imburfed a fingle *obolus*.   Nor did GUTENBERG
(who perfifted in his fruitlefs endeavours) reap any advantage from them ; for, when he quitted Strafburgh, he was
overwhelmed in debt, and under a neceffity of felling every
thing he was in poffeffion of.   See MEERMAN, vol. I. p.
198—202.   All the depofitions in the law-fuit abovementioned (with the judicial decree) are printed by Mr.
MEERMAN, vol. II. p. 58—88.   N.

1. WIM-

1. WIMPHELINGIUS [HH], the oldeſt writer in favour of Straſburg, tells us, that GUTENBERG was the inventor of *a new art of writing, ars impreſſoria,* which might almoſt be called a divine benefit, and which he happily completed at Mentz; but does not mention one book of his printing : though he adds, that MENTELIUS printed many volumes correctly and beautifully, and acquired great wealth: whence we may conclude that he perfected what GUTENBERG had in vain eſſayed.

2. WIMPHELINGIUS, in another book [II], tells us, the art of Printing was found out by GUTENBERG *incompletè* ; which implies, not that he practiſed the art in an imperfect manner (as LAURENTIUS had done at Harleim) but rather that he had not been able to accompliſh what he aimed at.

3. GUTENBERG, when he left Straſburg in 1444 or the following year, and entered into partnerſhip with GEINSFLEICH ſenior and others, had occaſion for his brother's aſſiſtance, to enable him to complete the art; which ſhews that his former attempts at Strasburgh had been unſucceſsful [KK].

4. Theſe particulars are remarkably confirmed by TRITHEMIUS, who tells us, in two different places [LL],

[HH] *Epitome rerum Germanicarum,* ed. Argent. 1505. MEERMAN, vol. I. p. 202. vol. II. p. 139.

[II] *Catal. Epiſc. Argentin.* 1508. MEERMAN, ut ſupra.

[KK] MEERMAN, ut ſupra.

[LL] *Annal. Hirſaug.* ut ſupra, and *Chron. Sponheim.* See MEERMAN, vol. II. p. 103. 127.

that

that GUTENBERG spent all his subsance in quest
of this art; and met with such insuperable difficulties, that, in despair, he had nearly given up all
hopes of attaining it, till he was assisted by the liberality of FUST, and by his brother's skill, in the
city of Mentz.

5. ULRIC ZELL says [MM], the art was completed
at Mentz; but that some books had been published
in Holland earlier than in that city. Is it likely that
ZELL, who was a German, would have omitted to
mention Strasburgh, if it had preceded Mentz in
Printing?

There is little doubt therefore that all GUTEN-
BERG's labours at Strasburgh amounted to no more
than a fruitless attempt, which he was at last under a
necessity of relinquishing: and there is no certain
proof of a single book having been printed in that city
till after the dispersion of the printers in 1462 [NN],

when

[MM] *Chronicon Coloniæ*, 1499. ZELL attributes the
invention to GUTENBERG at Mentz; whence, he says, the
art was first communicated to Cologn, next to Stratburgh,
and then to Venice. See MEERMAN, vol. II, p. 105.

[NN] From this period, Printing made a rapid progress
in most of the principal towns of Europe, as will appear by
an inspection of our Appendix, N° IV. In 1490, it reached
Constantinople; and, according to Mr. PALMER, p. 281,
&c. it was extended, by the middle of the next century, to
Africa and America. It was introduced into Russia about
1560; but, from motives either of policy or superstition,
it was speedily suppressed by the ruling powers; and, even

under

when MENTELIUS and EGGESTENIUS fuccefsfully purfued the bufinefs. The former indeed is fuppofed by
fome writers to have begun printing about the year
1447; but no fufficient authority appears for fuch
an affertion.

Having mentioned MENTELIUS, let us examine for
a moment how he comes to be confidered as the inventor of Printing. The origin of the art was known to
very few. The advocates for Mentz were divided
in their fentiments between GUTENBERG and FUST.
The city of Strasburgh put in its own claim to the
invention ; and GUTENBERG's failure of fuccefs
there, cutting off his pretence to the honour of it,
opened a way for MENTELIUS, who certainly was the
firft who publifhed books in that city. JOHN SCHOT-

under the prefent enlightened Emprefs, has fcarcely emerged
from its obfcurity.—That it was early practifed in the in-
hofpitable regions of Iceland, we have the authority of the
ingenious Mr. BRYANT : " ARNGRIM JONAS was born
" amidft the fnows of *Iceland*; yet as much prejudiced in
" favour of his country as thofe who are natives of an
" happier climate. This is vifible in his *Crymogæa*; but
" more particularly in his *Anatome Blefkiniana*. I have
" in my poffeffion this curious little treatife, written in
" Latin by him in his own country, and printed *Typis Ho-*
" *lenfibus in Iflandiâ Boreali, anno* 1612. *Hola* is placed in
" fome maps within the *Arctic* Circle, and is certainly not
" far removed from it. I believe, it is the fartheft North of
" any place, where Arts and Sciences have ever refided."
*Obfervations and Inquiries relating to various parts of Ancient
Hiflory,* 1767, p. 277. B. & N.

TUS,

TUS, a son of MENTELIUS's daughter, settled there
in 1510, after having resided at Friburg in Basil, and
took an opportunity of cultivating a report which was
likely to prove so advantageous to him among his
countrymen. He was more particularly excited to
this, by JOHN SCHOEFFER, of Mentz; who boasted
in his colophons, though not quite consistently with
truth, that JOHN FUST, his grandfather by the mother's side, was the first inventor [OO]. As Strasburgh
rivaled Mentz in its claim, why should SCHOTTUS give
place to SCHOEFFER, or why MENTELIUS to FUST?
If SCHOEFFER used artifice on one side, SCHOTTUS

[OO] JOHN SCHOEFFER was the first who attributed the
invention to FUST; not, as other writers do, by saying
that he assisted the first printers with money and advice;
but ascribes it to *his own ingenuity*. He did not, however, venture to assert so much at once, but artfully proceeded to it by degrees. In his first colophon, 1503, he
ascribes it *majoribus suis*, without naming them. In a dedication to the Emperor MAXIMILIAN, in 1505, he inge-
nuously calls GUTENBERG the inventor, and FUST and
SCHOEFFER the improvers. In 1509, he calls his grandfather *inventorem auctoremque*; and in 1515, in the colophon
to TRITHEMIUS, which is above cited, he asserts that FUST
completed the art with the assistance of PETER SCHOEFFER.
By a continual repetition of colophons to this purpose,
many were persuaded that the assertion was true, and
among others, it seems, the Emperor MAXIMILIAN ((see
above, p. 14); to whom, however, in 1505, JOHN
SCHOEFFER had given a very different account. See
MEERMAN, vol. II. p 144. N.

shewed

shewed more on the other. The former, without any
teftimony but his own repeated confident affertions,
drew over many in favour of Fust, leaving Gutenberg out of the queftion; and, among the reft,
even the Emperor Maximilian, who, in 1518,
granted Schoeffer *an exclufive privilege* of printing
Livy. Schottus was filent while this Emperor lived;
but no fooner was he dead, than he endeavoured to
perfuade his fucceffor Charles V, and the reft of the
learned world, that Fust fhould be divefted of his
imaginary claims, and Mentelius be put in his
place. To this purpofe, from the year 1520, he
prefixed his family arms to all the books he printed,
which had been granted, by Frederick III, to his
grandfather and defcendants; adding to them an infcription, " that they were granted to John Men-
" telius, *the firft inventor of Printing.*" But the
truth is, coat-armour had before been granted by that
emperor to the *typothetæ* and the *typographi*, to perpe-
tuate the difcovery [PP]; but to Mentelius he
granted them only as a private man who was defirous
of nobility, and the diploma contained not a word of
the invention of Printing: nor did Schottus dare
openly to affert that it was granted to Mentelius
for the invention of the art, left he fhould be detected
in a falfehood; but was content, by ufing an ambi-
guous expreffion, to miflead inattentive readers [QQ].

[PP] See above, p. 69, note [F].
[QQ] Meerman, vol. I. p. 205. & feqq.

A P P E N D I X.

N° I.

On the firft-printed GREEK Books.

IT cannot be thought foreign to our plan, to give a fhort account of the invention of thofe *charaƈters* by which the learned languages have been perpetuated, and particularly the Greek and Hebrew.

The firft effays in GREEK that can be difcovered are in the few fentences which occur in the famous edition of TULLY's *Offices*, 1465, at Mentz, which we have defcribed above; but thefe were miferably incorreƈt and barbarous, if we may judge from the fpecimens Mr. MAITTAIRE has given us [*a*], of which the following is one :

Οτίϲαταακαρτμακατα καὶ τατωτωκα.

In the fame year, 1465, was publifhed an edition of LACTANTIUS's *Inftitutes*, printed *in monafterio Sublacenfi*, in the kingdom of Naples, in which the quotations from the Greek authors are printed in a very neat Greek letter [*b*]. Mr. MEERMAN obferves,

[*a*] Vol. I. p. 61. & Pars pofterior, p. 274.
[*b*] PALMER, Hift. of Printing, p. 124.

that there is *a very ſtriking difference* between the Greek uſed in *Lactantius* and that of *Mentz*; as there is alſo in the types with which *the Latin* is printed. They ſeem to have had but *a very ſmall quantity* of Greek in the monaſtery; for, in the firſt part of the work, whenever a long ſentence occurred, a blank was left, that it might be written in with a pen; after the middle of the work, however, all the Greek that occurs is printed [*c*].

The firſt printers who ſettled at Rome were CONRAD SWEYNHEIM and ARNOLD PANNARTZ, who introduced the preſent *Roman* type, in 1467, in CICERO's *Epiſtolæ Familiares*: in 1469 they printed a beautiful edition of AULUS GELLIUS, with the Greek quotations in a fair character, without accents or ſpirits, and with very few abbreviations [*d*].

It

[*c*] Before this period, the uniform character was the old *Gothic*, or *German*; whence our *Black* was afterwards formed. But *Lactantius* is printed in a kind of Semi-gothic, of great elegance, and approaching nearly to the preſent *Roman* type; which laſt was firſt uſed at Rome in 1467, and ſoon after brought to great perfection in Italy, particularly by JENSON. MEERMAN, vol. II. p. 248.

[*d*] After having printed, in ſix or ſeven years at moſt, a great number of very beautiful and correct editions, theſe ingenious printers were reduced to the moſt neceſſitous circumſtances. Their learned patron the Biſhop of ALERIA (who was the editor of AULUS GELLIUS) preſented a petition to Pope Sixtus IV, in 1471, in behalf of " theſe
" worthy

It appears then that some confiderable fragments of Greek were very early introduced into printed books; but the firft whole book that is yet known is the Greek Grammar of CONSTANTINE LASCARIS, in quarto, revifed by DEMETRIUS CRETENSIS, and printed by DIONYSIUS PALAVISINUS, at Milan, 1476 [*e*].

" worthy and induftrious printers;" in which he reprefents their great merit and mifery in the moft pathetic terms; and declares their readinefs to part with their whole ftock for fubfiftence. " We were the firft of the Germans (they " fay) who introduced this art, with vaft labour and coft, " into your Holinefs's territories, in the time of your pre- " deceffor: and encouraged, by our example, other printers " to do the fame. If you perufe the catalogue of the " works printed by us, you will admire how and where we " could procure a fufficient quantity of paper, or even rags, " for fuch a number of volumes.—The total of thefe " books amounts to 12,475, a prodigious heap, and into- " lerable to us, your Holinefs's printers, by reafon of thofe " unfold. We are no longer able to bear the great ex- " pence of houfe-keeping, for want of buyers; of which " there cannot be a more flagrant proof, than that our " houfe, though otherwife fpacious enough, is full of " *Quire-books,* but void of every neceffary of life." The curious Reader may fee the whole of this interefting pe- tition, which is dated March 1, 1472, with the catalogue of their books, in PALMER, p. 130, &c. who has tranflated it from CHEVILLIER. See alfo MAITTAIRE, vol. I. p. 46. & Pars pofterior, p. 276.

[*e*] PALMER, p. 215.

In

In 1481, the Greek *Pfalter* was printed in that city, with a Latin tranflation, in folio [*f*].

Venice [*g*] foon followed the example of Milan; and in 1486 were publifhed in that city the *Greek Pfalter*, and the *Batrachomyomachia*, the former by ALEXANDER, the latter by LAONICUS, both natives of Crete. They were printed in a very uncommon character; the latter of them with *accents* and *fpirits*, and alfo with *fcholia* [*h*].

In

[*f*] LE LONG, Bibliotheca Sacra, p. 436. A fine copy of this edition is now in the poffeffion of the Rev. Mr. DE MISSY, purchafed by that Gentleman, with many other valuable books, at the fale of the Harleian Library.

[*g*] In an edition of PLINY's Natural Hiftory, printed by Jo. DE SPIRA in 1469 (fee above, p. 45), a Greek infcription, l. vii. c. 58, is thus miferably mif-printed in Roman letters, "xixilipcui canece comai cockpturæ trata una ciezica," inftead of Ναυσικράτης Τισαμένε Ἀθηναῖ᭢ Κόρη ᵹ Ἀθηνᾷ ἀνέθηκεν. CHISHULL, Antiq. Afiat. p. 20. A copy of this edition (which HARDUIN feems not to have known of, and which is the more valuable for preferving this figual mark of ignorance in the editor) was in Dr. MEAD's magnificent library; whence it afterwards came into the curious collection of another Gentleman who was equally an ornament to Literature and to Medicine, the late learned Dr. ASKEW. This book, containing 750 pages was printed in the fhort fpace of three months. See MEERMAN, vol. I. p. 15.

[*h*] MAITTAIRE, vol. I. p. 182.—" If MAITTAIRE left " it a matter of doubt whether the Pfalter has *accents* and " *fpirits*, it muft be becaufe he had not feen the book : for it " has them certainly in my copy, nor do I remember they

P   " were

In 1488, however, all former publications in this language were eclipfed by a fine edition of HOMER's works at Florence, in folio, printed by DEMETRIUS, a native of *Crete*. Thus Printing (fays Mr. MAITTAIRE, p. 185.) feems to have attained its ἀκμὴ of perfection, after having exhibited moſt beautiful fpecimens of Latin, Greek, and Hebrew. (See *Appendix*, Nº II.)

In 1493, a fine edition of ISOCRATES was printed at *Milan*, in folio, by HENRY GERMAN and SEBASTIAN EX PANTREMULO. (See PALMER, p. 158.)

All the above works are prior in time to thofe of ALDUS, who has been erroneouſly fuppofed to be the *firſt* Greek Printer; yet the beauty, correctneſs, and

" were wanting in the only one I ever faw befides, I mean the
" copy which, if I miſtake not, was purchaſed for three
" guineas and a half by Dr. ASKEW from Dr. MEAD's Li-
" brary. As to the *Types* (whether caſt or cut, for I have
" fome fcruples about it) they may be called a rough, though
" not altogether unlike imitation of thofe MſſT. *medii ævi*, fuch
" as fome in my poſſeſſion, which I look upon as written by
" a purely Greek hand, and not with a pen, but with a reed.
" I had formerly (but gave them to Dr. ASKEW, who in re-
" turn *promiſed* me fome other trifling literary favour) a few
" leaves of an ancient printed book which I gueſſed was LAS-
" CARIS's or GAZA's Greek Grammar; and the impreſſion
" of which, as it then feemed to me, refembled very much
" *that* of the Pfalter in queſtion. A more imperfect refem-
" blance of its coeval *Batrachomyomachia*, may be feen in the
" engraved fpecimen of it which was drawn, I fuppofe, by
" MAITTAIRE himfelf, and publifhed with his edition of
" that Poem, *anno* 1721." C. D. M.

3   number

number of his editions place him in a much higher rank than his predeceffors. His characters were more beautiful and elegant than any before ufed. He was born in 1445, and died in 1515 [*n*].

This article fhould clofe here; but it would be unpardonable not to mention the celebrated ROBERT STEPHENS and his fon HENRY; whofe impreffions, in Hebrew, Greek, and Latin, are well known. Though the noble Greek books of ALDUS had raifed an univerfal defire of reviving that tongue, the French were backward in introducing it. The only pieces printed by them were fome quotations, fo wretchedly performed, that they were rather to be gueffed at than read [*o*];

[*n*] ALDUS was the inventor of the *Italic* character which is now in ufe, called, from his name, *Aldine*, or *Curfivus*. This fort of letter he contrived, to prevent the great number of abbreviations that were then in ufe; a fingular fpecimen of which is preferved by CHEVILLIER, p. 110: Si hic ε fæl sm q̃d ad fimplr ã e p̃ducibile a deo g̃ α ε̃ & str hic a η̃ ε̃ g̃ a η̃ ε̃ p̃ducibile a deo, &c. *i. e.* "Sicut hic eft fallacia fecundum quid ad fimpliciter A "eft producibile a deo: Ergo A eft. Et fimiliter hic. A non "eft: Ergo non eft producibile a deo." PALMER, p. 151, 152. MAITTAIRE, vol. I. p. 237.

[*o*] This is faid on the authority of PALMER, p. 270.— " The father of ROBERT was alfo named HENRY, and was " perhaps the firft that began to print Greek quotations in " fuch a manner that they could not be faid to be *wretchedly* " *performed, and rather to be gueffed at than read.* I judge of " this by his edition of *Fabri Stapulenfis Quincuplex Pfalterium*, " printed at Paris, and publifhed in 1513." C. D. M.

in

in a character very rude and uncouth, and without accents. But Francis Tissard, in 1507, introduced the study of this language at Paris, where the printing of it was fuccefsfully practised till brought to the highest perfection by Robert and Henry Stephens.

The first Greek edition of the *whole Bible* was printed at *Complutum*, under the care of Cardinal Ximenes [*p*]; but as this edition, though finished

in

[*p*] See our Appendix, N° III. p. 128. And fee an account of all the early Greek and Latin editions both of the Old and New Teftament in Le Long's Bibliotheca Sacra. — Mr. Maittaire, however, Annal. Typogr. t. I. p. 41, mentions a Latin Bible, of Paris, unnoticed by Le Long, which is without a date; but is fixed by [Mr. Barricave] a learned friend of Mr. Maittaire's to the year 1464, the third year of the reign of Louis XI, from the three following verfes printed in a colophon at the end of it:

" Jam femi undecimus luftrum Francos Ludovicus

" Rexerat, Ulricus, Martinus, itémque Michael

" Orti Teutoniâ hanc mihi compofuere figuram."

Mr. Palmer, Hift. of Printing, p. 100, after citing the above conjecture, adds, " I am perfuaded that Mr. Mait-
" taire's friend was miftaken in the firft verfe. As Che-
" villier gives us the fame colophon at the end of the
" firft Paris Bible by the fame three partners, with this va-
" riation however from the former, that inftead of *femi*
" *luftrum*, it has *tribus luftris*, that is, inftead of the *third*,
" it imports the *thirteenth* year of that King's reign: we
" may eafily fuppofe, that it was the firft Paris Bible of
" 1475; and this Gentleman might probably be miftaken:
" however, the book being in Queen's College library, in
" Cam-

in 1517, was not publiſhed till 1522, that of *Venice*, 1518, may properly be called the firſt edition of the whole Greek Bible, though Erasmus had publiſhed the New Teſtament, at Baſil, in 1516.

" Cambridge, it may be eaſily conſulted." We have the authority of the very learned and accurate Dr. Taylor in Mſ. to aſſert, that " Mr. Maittaire's friend was not miſtaken. " The verſes are as quoted by Mr. Maittaire, *ſemi luſtrum,* " not *tribus luſtris;*" and, that " the book is not in Queen's " College Library, but in the Library of the Univerſity, in " that part of it which was given by King George I."—We ſhall juſt mention occaſionally, as it falls in our way, another very ſcarce Latin Bible publiſhed by Servetus, whence Dr. Gregory Sharpe cites a note of Servetus, in his *Second Argument,* &c. and of which he ſays, p. 254, *The Jeſuits at Lions, when I enquired after this book, did not know that it ever had been publiſhed: and Mr. Arkenholtz, a very learned and ingenious man, the librarian at Heſſe Caſſel, where the works of Servetus are ſuppoſed to be preſerved, though the* Christianismus Restitutus *is loſt, having been ſtolen out of the library, when the Landgrave himſelf was preſent, did not, till I convinced him, believe that Servetus ever publiſhed an edition of the Bible.* In Dr. Mead's Catalogue, p. 3, this edition is intituled, *Biblia Sacra ex Pagnini tranſlatione, per* Mich. Villanovanum, i. e. Servetum, *Lugduni,* 1542, *folio.* B. & N.—" If Dr. " Sharpe's intention in this note was only, as I ſuppoſe, to " make his Readers ſenſible how ſcarce a book that Bible is " from which he quoted a paſſage, it may be but ſeconding his " intention to obſerve, that *his* copy, Dr. Mead's copy, and " *my* copy of it, are but *one: his* copy being that which he had " borrowed of me, and *mine* being no other than Dr. Mead's; " which I purchaſed when his library was ſold by auction in " 1754." C. D. M.—For Seven Pounds, as appea s by a Catalogue in which the prices are marked. N.   N°

Nᵒ II.

On the firſt-printed HEBREW Books:
with Obſervations on ſome modern Editions;
and a Collation, from WALTON's Polyglott,
of a remarkable paſſage, as printed in *Kings*
and *Chronicles.*

A VERY ſatisfactory account of this branch of
Printing is thus given by a Gentleman whoſe learned
labours have for many years been conſtantly employed in elucidating the Hebrew Scriptures [a]:

" The method which ſeems to have been originally
" obſerved, in printing the Hebrew Bible, was juſt
" what might have been expected:

" I. The PENTATEUCH, in 1482 [b].

" II. The PRIOR PROPHETS, in 1484 [c].

[a] Dr. KENNICOTT, in *Ten Annual Accounts of the Collation of Hebrew Mſſ.* p. 112. In the Doctor's Plan for printing a corrected Bible (dated Dec. 16, 1772) an edition of
the *Pſalms* is mentioned, ſo early as 1477.

[b] A copy of this edition is preſerved at Verona. Another copy of it is in the curious Library of the Margravo
of BADEN DURLAC. *Annual Accounts,* p. 112.

[c] This edition (containing *Joſhua, Judges,* and *Samuel*)
Dr. KENNICOTT ſaw in the Royal Library at Paris. Ibid.

" III.

" III. The Posterior Prophets, in 1486 [*d*].

" IV. The Hagiographa, in 1487 [*e*].

" And, after the Four great parts had been thus
" printed feparately (each with a comment), The
" whole Text (without a comment) was printed in
" one volume in 1488 [*f*] : and the text continued to be
" printed,

[*d*] This edition contained the *Prophetæ priores* and *pofte-riores,* according to Wolfius, Biblioth. Hebraica, vol. II. p. 397. See Dr. Kennicott's State of the printed Hebrew Text, Differt. II. p. 472. It was printed at *Soncino,* in the dutchy of Milan, without vowel points, cum Com. David Kimchi, fol. See Le Long, Bibliotheca Sacra, p. 129; and Palmer, p. 249.

[*e*] Printed at Naples in 1487. A copy of the *Hagiographa,* in two volumes, on vellum, was prefented by Dr. Pellet to Eaton College Library. It contains many curious read-ings, different from all the other printed copies, and con-trary to the *Mafora.* The laft is probably one of the rea-fons for which the whole edition may have been deftroyed excepting this copy, which had the fingular good fortune to efcape the flames. Dr. Pellet fays, *Hoc exemplar uni-cum, & flammis ereptum, uti par eft credere.* This edition however is printed with the vowel points, except one whole page of *Daniel.* See Dr. Kennicott, Diff. I. p. 521. Diff. II. p. 473.—Another copy has been fince difcovered, in the *Cafanatenfian* library at Rome. *Annual Collations,* p. 112.

[*f*] Printed at Soncino, with vowel points, by Abra-ham fil. Rabbi Hhajim, fol. See Le Long, p. 96, where is a particular enumeration of all the principal editions till the year 1709. The whole of the *New Teftament* was firft publifhed

" printed, as in thefe firft editions, fo in feveral others
" for twenty or thirty years, without marginal *Keri*
" or *Mafora*, and with greater agreement to the more
" antient Mff.; till, about the year 1520, fome of
" the Jews adopted *later* Mff. and the *Mafora*; which
" abfurd preference has obtained ever fince."

Thus much for the *ancient* editions given by Jews.

In 1742, a Hebrew Bible was printed at Mantua,
under the care of the moft learned Jews in Italy.
This Bible had not been heard of among the Chri-
ftians in this country, nor perhaps in any other;
though the nature of it is very extraordinary. The
text indeed is nearly the fame with that in other
modern editions: but at the bottom of each page
are Various Readings, amounting in the whole to
above 2000, and many of them of great confequence,
collected from Mff. printed editions, copies of the

publifhed in Hebrew by ELIAS HUTTER in 1599, in a
Polyglott edition, which will be defcribed in our Appendix, N° III. B. & N.—" But long enough before this, at
" Bafil, anno 1537, was publifhed *(typis* HENRICI PETRI)
" a fmall folio, containing a pretended antient Gofpel of *St.*
" *Matthew* in Hebrew, together with a Latin Tranflation,
" and Annotations by the Editor SEBASTIANUS MUN-
" STERUS; the fame who, anno 1535, had publifhed an
" Hebrew Bible, with a new Latin Tranflation of his own,
" and Annotations, at Bafil, in two volumes in folio: which
" were reprinted at Bafil with confiderable improvements,
" anno 1546. Of this I have a fine copy." C. D. M.

Talmud,

Talmud, and the works of the moſt renowned Rab-
bies.   And in one of the notes is this remark:—
" That in ſeveral paſſages of the Hebrew Bible the
" differences are ſo many and ſo great, that they know
" not which to fix upon as the true Readings [g]."

We cannot quit this ſubjeſt without obſerving,
on Dr. KENNICOTT's authority, that as the firſt
printed Bibles are more correſt than the later
ones, ſo the variations between the firſt edition,
printed in 1488, and the edition of VANDER
HOOGHT, in 1705, at Amſterdam, in 2 vols, 8vo,
amount upon the whole, to above TWELVE
THOUSAND! [h]

But theſe are not the only Variations that we
are concerned to take notice of.   Parallel places of
Scripture, though evidently derived from the ſame
original, are found to differ in no ſmall degree.   Of
this many ſtriking inſtances have been long ſince given
by Dr. KENNICOTT, in his *State of the printed Hebrew Text*, Diff. I.   And we are enabled, by the
kindneſs of a valuable Friend, to lay before the
Reader another ſpecimen of the ſame kind, in a
Collation of the accounts of the Dedication of the
Temple, as written 1 Kings vii. 51. viii. 1, &c. and
2 Chron. v. 1, &c.

[g] Dr. KENNICOTT's Plan, Dec. 16, 1772.
[h] Annual Accounts, p. 130.

Q   A C O L-

A COLLATION
OF THE ACCOUNT OF
The DEDICATION of the TEMPLE.

1 Kings vii.	2 Chron. v.

VARIOUS READINGS.

Ver. 51. הַמֶּלֶךְ . . .	Ver. 1. wanting.
בית falfely for . .	לבית
דוד . . .	דויד
את הכסף . . .	ואת הכסף wrong.
ואת הכלים . .	ואת כל הכלים
יהוה . .	האלהים
viii. 1. יקהל . .	2. יקהיל
הַמֶּלֶךְ שְׁלֹמֹה re-dundant.	wanting
דוד, . . .	דויד
2. שלמה . .	3. wanting.
בירה האתנים	improperly omitted.
3. הכהנים . .	4. הלוים
4. את ארון יהוה	5. את הארון without יהוה
ויעלו . .	העלו
והלוים rightly.	הלוים
5. אתו redundant.	6. wanting.
6. ויבאו . .	7. ויביאו
הכרובים . .	הכרובים .
7. כי . . .	8. ויהיו
אל . . .	על
ויסכו lit. tranſpoſitis.	ויכסו
הכרבים . .	הכרובים
8. ויאריכו . .	9. ויאריכו
הקדש . .	הארון
ויהיו rightly. .	ויהי
9. להות האבנים . .	*10. הלחות without האבנים

* N. B. בְּרִית ſeems to be wanting in both places after כָּרַת.

1.Kings viii.   2 Chron. v. and vi.

VARIOUS READINGS.

1 Kings viii.	2 Chron. v. and vi.
‏9. הנח‎ ל	‏10. נתן‎ ל
‏שם‎ rightly	negligently omitted.
‏מארץ מצרים‎	‏ממצרים‎
‏10. והענן מלא את בית יהוה‎	‏13. בית * ענן מלא והבית יהוה‎
‏11. את בית יהוה‎	‏14. את בית האלהים‎
‏13. בנה‎	‏vi. 2. ואני‎
‏מכון‎	‏ומכון‎
‏14. עמד‎	‏3. עומד‎
‏15. דוד‎	‏4. דויד‎
‏ובידו‎	‏ובידיו‎
‏16. את ישראל‎	5. wanting.
‏ממצרים‎	‏מארץ מצרים.‎

N. B. The oppofite 13 words, though neceffary to complete the fenfe, are omitted in Kings, owing to the fimilar endings of two fentences, one of which the tranfcriber negligently overlooked.

‏ולא בחרתי באיש להיות נגיד על עמי ישראל : ואבחר בירושלם להיות שמי שם —‎

1 Kings viii.	2 Chron. vi.
‏16. בדוד‎	‏6. בדויד‎
‏17. דוד‎	‏7. דויד‎
‏18. דוד‎	‏8. דויד‎
‏הטיבת‎	‏הטיבות‎
‏19. כי אם‎	‏9. כי'‎ without ‏אם‎
‏20. ואקם‎	‏10. ואקום‎
‏דוד‎	‏ודויד‎
‏21. ואשם‎	‏11. ואשים‎
‏מקום לארון‎	‏את־הארון‎
‏אבתינו‎	‏בני ישראל‎
‏בהוציאו אתם מארץ מצרים‎	wanting.

* For ‏בית‎ the LXX read ‏כבוד‎. The text is evidently wrong; and ought to ftand as in 1 Kings.

Q 2

ỳ 22.

1 Kings viii.   2 Chron. vi.

VARIOUS READINGS.

1 Kings viii.	2 Chron. vi.
℣ 22. שלמה	℣ 12. wanting.
השמים	* 13. השמימה
23. אלהים	14. האלהים
ממעל	wanting.
ועל הארץ	ובארץ
מתחת	wanting.
24. דוד	15. דויד
25. דוד	16. דויד
ישב	יושב
לפני	בתורתי
26. אלהי	17. יהיה אלהי
נא	wanting.
דבריך wrong.	דברך right.
דוד אבי	לדויד
27. wanting.	18. את האדם
השמים	שמים
יכלכלך	יכלכלוך
28. היום	19. wanting.
29. עינך	20. עיניך
פתחת	פתוחות
לילה ויום	יומם ולילה
יהיה שמי	לשום שמך
לשמע	לשמוע
30. תחנת	21. תהניני
אל מקום	ממקום
אל השמים	מן השמים
31. את אשר	22. אם
32. השמים	23. מן השמים
להרשיע רשע	להשיב לרשע
33. בהנגף	24. ואם ינגף
אשר	כי

* Verse 13th is a parenthesis (not extant in Kings) with part of verse 12th repeated.

℣ 33

1 Kings viii.	2 Chron. vi.

VARIOUS READINGS.

1 Kings viii.	2 Chron. vi.
33. אליך ע	24. wanting. ע
אליך	לפניך
34. השמים	25. מן השמים
והשבתם	והשיבותם
נתת לאבותם	נתתה להם ולאבתיהם
35. שמים	26. השמים
ומחטאתם	מחטאתם
36. את הדרך	27. אל הדרך
37. ירקון	28. וירקון right.
איבו	איבי wrong.
כל מחלה	וכל מחלה right.
38. תהיה	29. יהיה
לכל עמך	ולכל עמך
ידעון	ידעו
נגע לבבו	נגעו ומכאבו
39. השמים	30. מן השמים
ועשית	wanting.
ונתת	ונתתה
ידעת לבדך	לבדך ידעת
כל בני	כל בני without
40. יראוך	31. ייראוך
wanting.	ללכת בדרכיך
42. כי ישמעון את שמך	32. wanting.
ואת ידך	וידך
וזרעך	וזרועך
ובא	ובאו
והתפלל	והתפללו
43. אתה	33. ואתה
השמים	מן השמים
מכום	ממכום
ידעון	ידעו
ליראה	וליראה
44. איבו	34. איביו

ע 44

1 Kings viii.	2 Chron. vi.

VARIOUS READINGS.

1 Kings viii.	2 Chron. vi.
44. אל יהוה	34. אליך
wanting.	הזאת
בנתי	בניתי
45. השמים	35. מן השמים
46. שביהם	36. שוביהם
האויב	wanting.
47. אל לבם	37. אל לבבם
שביהם	שבים
והעוינו	העוינו right.
רשענו	ורשענו right.
48. לבבם	38. לבם
איביהם	שבים
אליך	wanting.
העיר	והעיר
והבית	ולבית
בנית	בניתי right.
49. השמים	39. מן השמים
מכון	ממכון
תחנתם	תחנתיהם

N. B. This Collation, made from WALTON's *Polyglott*, proceeds no farther, becaufe the remainder of SOLOMON's Prayer is very different in *Kings*, from what it is in *Chronicles*; for which difference if the Learned could clearly account, it would be of great fervice to this important branch of Literature.

In

In Mr. CLARKE's *Connexion of the Roman, Saxon, and English Coins,* among many other interesting particulars, is a curious Differtation on the *Jewish Money;* in which the *Shekel,* as determined by GRSEPSIUS*, is proved (against the united authority of VILLALPANDUS and GREAVES) to have been fynonymous to the *Didrachma,* or forty-eighth part of a pound : and confequently a fourth part of an ounce ; not half an ounce, as has been commonly fuppofed.

* " It is now almoſt two centuries fince STANISLAUS GRSEPSIUS, a learned Polander, publifhed a treatife, *De multiplici ficlo, et talento Hebraico.* This book met with a very fingular fate. It was at firſt much neglected, and then, about a century afterwards, publifhed in Germany, as a very choice Mſ. found in one of their libraries. One HENRICUS GOUTIER THULEMARIUS reprinted it word for word, without taking the leaſt notice of its author ; and this Literary Pirate was in time regarded.as the true Proprietor. See BAUDELOT, Utilité des Voyages, vol. II. p. 247. and FABRICIUS, Bibl. Ant. p. 27." Mr. CLARKE, p. 242.—This learned work of GRSEPSIUS would not be a temptation to a Literary Pirate of thefe days !

N° III.

N° III.

On the firſt-printed POLYGLOTTS.

THE firſt POLYGLOTT work was printed at Genoa
in 1516, by PETER PAUL PORRUS [a], who under-
took to print the Pentaglott Pſalter of AUGUSTIN JU-
STINIAN, biſhop of Nebo.   It was in Hebrew, Arabic [b], Chaldaic, and Greek, with the Latin Verſions,
Gloſſes,

[a] " By PORRUS it was *printed* at Genoa, *in ædibus*
" *Nicolai* JUSTINIANI *Pauli* ; whither he ſeems to have
" been invited for that purpoſe : after which I conceive
" that he returned to his uſual place of abode at Turin ;
" as by himſelf, at the end of the book, he is called *Petrus*
" *Porrus Mediolanenſis* TAURINI DEGENS."   C. D. M.

[b] The Arabic verſion is of no authority, as it was
tranſlated, not from the Hebrew, but from the Septuagint ;
where the verſion of the Prophets (particularly *Jeremiah*) is
leſs faithful than that of the other books of the Old Teſtament, and was probably made by a Jew who was very ignorant
of Hebrew.   But this is very far from being the caſe of the
Pentateuch. See MICHAELIS, *Syntagma Commentationum*,
1763, Comm. III. p. 58. and PRIDEAUX, vol. II. folio, p. 36.
The Illyrian, Gothic, Arabic, Ethiopic, Armenian, and
Syriac verſions were all made from the Septuagint ; though
there is ſtill in being an older verſion of the Syriac, tranſlated
immediately from the Hebrew original. PRIDEAUX, p. 37.
  " The Arabic is the *lateſt* of all the antient verſions of
" the Old Teſtament.—In the year 942 died R. SAADIAS,
" called

Gloſſes, and Scholia, which laſt made the eighth column, in *folio*. The *Arabic* was the firſt that ever was printed, and this the firſt piece of the Bible that ever appeared in ſo many languages [*b*].

In

" called *Gaon* (i. e. *the illuſtrious*), who preſided over the
" Babylonian ſchools.—The chief merit of this learned and
" laborious Rabbi is, that he tranſlated all the Old Teſta-
" ment from the Hebrew into Arabic ; expreſſing the Ara-
" bic in Hebrew characters. But though the whole He-
" brew Bible was thus tranſlated by him ; yet *the Penta-*
" *teuch* only has been, as yet, publiſhed from his verſion.
" The other books, now in Arabic, in the Paris and Lon-
" don Polyglotts, were tranſlated at different times, by dif-
" ferent authors ; partly from the Greek, and partly from
" the Syriac verſions : and but few parts, if any, (except-
" ing the Pentateuch) were tranſlated from the Hebrew."
Dr. KENNICOTT, on the State of the printed Hebrew Text, Diſſ. II. p. 452—454.

See a particular enumeration of the Arabic verſions, both Mſ. and printed, in LE LONG, p. 214, &c.

[*b*] JUSTINIAN, preſuming this work would procure him great gain, as well as reputation, cauſed 2000 copies to be printed of it, and promiſed in his Preface to proceed with the other parts of the Bible. But he was miſerably diſappointed : every body applauded the work ; but few proceeded further ; and ſcarce a fourth part of his number was ſold. Beſides the 2000 copies, he had alſo printed fifty upon vellum, which he preſented to all the kings, whether Chriſtians or Infidels. The whole New Teſtament was prepared for the preſs by JUSTINIAN, who had alſo made

R   great

In 1518, John Potken publifhed the Pfalter, in
Hebrew, Greek, Latin, and Æthiopic, [or Chaldaic,
as he, with fome others, called it,] at Cologn; but the
name of the Printer is no where to be found throughout the book [*c*]. It has no Preface properly fo
called :

great progrefs in the Old. See Le Long, Bibliotheca Sacra,
p. 2. Maittaire, Annal. Typ. tom. II. Par. I. p. 121.
Palmer, Hift. of Printing, p. 263.

[*c*] The *Printer's* name is no where mentioned, that we
know of, except in the following obfervations of the Reverend C. De-Missy, to whom this article had been communicated : 'I would almoft venture to affirm, that *you* have
' named him when you named *Potken.* For if he does not
' fay exprefily that *he* was the Printer, he feems at leaft to
' give us a broad hint of it, when he fays : *Statui jam*
' *fenex linguas externas aliquas difcere : & per artem impreffo-*
' *riam, quam adolefcens* didici, *edere : ut modico ære libri in*
' *diverfis linguis, formis æncis excufi emi poffint.* Thefe words
' might have been minded, but were omitted, by *Le Long*
' in the abftracts he made of Potken's addrefs to his
' readers at the end of the book. Towards the end of the
' fame Addrefs he fays *imprimi curavi :* but fuch a phrafe
' may very well be underftood of one who faw his work
' printed at home with his own types. And befides, he
' might have chofen that phrafe as the moft convenient, on
' account of his having been abfent for fome time while
' the impreffion was carried on by his kinfman and learned
' affiftant *Soter,* alias *Heyl.* Confer with the above Addrefs
' what he fays, p. 7. (col. 2 *fub finem*) of his *Introductiun-*
' *culae,* &c. a fmall work of no more than four leaves,
' which was certainly intended to go along with the Pfalter,
' though

called: But from an Addrefs of POTKEN to the ftu-
dious Readers, which is printed on the laft page of the
Pfalter,

' though it is not always, and is perhaps very feldom,
' to be found with it. In the abovementioned Addrefs he
' pretends to be the firft who had *imported into Europe* what
' he calls *the Chaldee* [now more properly called the
' *Æthiopic*] *Tongue.* And nothing hitherto has appeared to
' the contrary. Some quibblers indeed might object, that
' it rather was imported by the Æthiopian Fryars who had
' helped him to learn it. But he certainly feems to have
' been the firft who prefented the European Republic of
' Letters with a printed *Introductiuncula* to the Reading of
' that language : nor could any body, that I know of, have
' faid in 1518, that in 1513 he had publifhed or printed an
' Æthiopic book in Europe, as Potken does in his Addrefs
' of 1518, where he acquaints us, that nearly five years
' before, he had given at Rome an edition of the Æthiopic
' Pfalter printed by itfelf : for it is evidently of fuch a
' Pfalter that he fays : *Pfalterium . . . . . arte impreffcria*
' *. . . . . . . quinquennio vix exacto, Romæ edidi :* which
' book is noticed by *Le Long,* in thefe words : *Pfalmi &*
' *Canticum Canticorum Æthiopice ftudio Joannis Potken cum*
' *ejus præfatione Latina, in* 4°. Romæ 1513. That *Latin*
' *Preface,* could I get a fight of it, would perhaps enable
' me to be more particular and more pofitive. The book
' is marked by Le Long himfelf as being in the Royal
' Library at Paris; and an account of the faid Preface,
' no-doubt, might eafily be obtained, if afking for it fhould
' become a matter of any importance to the curious. Thus
' much, however, I thought, might be propofed provi-
' fionally, concerning the name of the Printer to whom

R 2 ' the

Pfalter, we are informed, that, while his earneft zeal
for Chriftianity, and for the Roman See, made him
extremely

' the world was indebted for Potken's Polyglott Pfalter.
' ———But fince I have dwelt fo long upon that fubject,
' I cannot well difmifs it without adding a word about the
' rank which Le Long gives to this work among the firft
' printed Polyglott Pfalters; immediately after that of *Juf-*
' *tiniani*, printed by *Porrus* in 15 6; and before another,
' by him fuppofed to be printed, as well as Potken's, two
' years later. *Pfalterium Hebraice, Græce, & Latine, curâ*
' *& ftudio Defid. Erafmi.* V. S. *Hieronymi Opera, in fol.*
' *Bafileæ, typis Amerbachii* 1518. Such was Le Long's in-
' dication of the book in the firft edition of his *Bibliotheca*
' *Sacra.* In the laft Paris edition (1723) it runs thus:
" Pfalterium Hebraice, & Latine, tam ex Verfione S.
" Hieronymi fecundum Hebraicam veritatem quam ex
" Vulgata Latina, cura & ftudio Defid. Erafmi & Conr.
" Pellicani. V. S. *Hieronymi Opera,* in fol. Bafileæ, typis
" Amerbachii 1518," and is followed by thefe fcraps *Ex*
' *præfatione Brunonis Amerbachii.* " Veteri probatæque
" Theologiæ plurimum lucis accefferum ex hac caftiffima
" [*it fhould have been* caftigatiffima] Hieronymianorum ope-
" rum editione, quam in primis Erafmo, nonnihil etiam nobis
" ftudiofi ferre debent acceptum [*for* acceptam] ... Nos huic
" octavo tomo corollarii vice quadruplex Pfalterium adje-
" cimus, videlicet & Hebraicum, & huic oppofitam D.
" [*divi*: Hieronymi verfionem, quam vulgo Hebræam ve-
" ritatem appellant, Græcum item, cui refpondet e regione
" trulatio quæ paffim legitur, ἀδηλ.ℌ᾽, hoc eft incerto auctore
" [*autore incerto*] ... & in Hebraicis præcipue curavimus,
" ut quam minimum ab archetypis & his antiquiffimis difce-
' deremus

extremely defirous of learning foreign languages,
efpecially what he calls the Chaldee, for which he
was

" deremus . . . . . Porro fatemur ingenue hoc negotii ἐκ
" ἀνευθησέως, [ἐκ ἄνευ ἑησέως,] quod aiunt, nos confeciffe,
" fed adjutus [*adjutos*] opera doctiffimi pariter & humaniffimi
" Patris Conradi [*Chonradi*] Pellicani Rubeaquenfis, ex
" familia D. [*divi*] Francifci, cujus aufpicio potiffimum hæc
" res peracta eft." What fhall we fay to all this? I have
' certainly ftrong reafons to queftion whether Le Long ever
' faw an edition of what is commonly called *Erafmus's St.*
' *Jerom,* bearing the date of 1518 : except fome copy or
' copies of the firft edition fhould be fuppofed to have been
' fold with a new title bearing fuch a date. But even this
' I have ftrong reafons to difbelieve. The moft, in fhort,
' I can grant is, that confidering the more general ufe, and
' of courfe the more general demand, of the eighth vo-
' lume, or even of the very feparable part of it which con-
' tains the Polyglott Pfalter ; fome copies of either may
' have been fold fingly with any frefher title and date, in
' order to pleafe that very common fort of buyers who will
' by all means be ferved with the neweft edition. A copy
' of the intire eighth volume I can fhew, the date of which,
' in the title page, is fo late as 1527. But then, on the very
' back of that title page, is printed a fhort Preface by
' Bruno Amerbachius, the original date of which is thus pre-
' ferved : *Idibus Januariis. Anno M.D.XVI:* and in which he
' declares that a peculiar Preface fhall be given to the Poly-
' glott Pfalter. Now this peculiar Preface is certainly the
' fame from which the above abftracts have been taken by
' Le Long : and being likewife printed on the back of the
' Pfalter's title-page, preferves alfo the original date of
                                                        ' the

was deftitute of any proper mafter; fome Æthiopian
Fryars happened to be at Rome, (as he expreffes it)
pere-

‘ the faid year 1516: from which circumftances, without
‘ defcending to more minute particulars, it is plain, I think,
‘ that this Pfalter, being two years more antient than Pot-
‘ ken’s, ought to have been placed before it. Nay, I would
‘ fain afk, if it might not difpute the precedency even with
‘ Porrus’s ? And this at leaft I can affirm, that Porrus’s
‘ date is *Menfe* VIIIIbri, and Amerbach’s VIII *Calend. Sep-*
‘ *tembreis.* Neither could it well be urged as a decifive
‘ point in favour of Porrus’s, that its date is at the end of
‘ the work, while Amerbach’s is only at the end of a Pre-
‘ face, on the very back of the title-page, which apparently
‘ was printed the firft of all, and that the time required to
‘ print the reft might retard the difpatch of the whole book
‘ beyond the month of November. For, not to mention
‘ the Printer’s well-known and almoft prodigious diligence,
‘ who, by taking proper meafures before-hand, and fetting
‘ feveral preffes at work for the fame book, might have done
‘ with it before the laft mentioned month ; it will be fuffi-
‘ cient to obferve, *in the firft place,* That the firft fheet of
‘ the firft *Quaternio,* though ready for the prefs, may have
‘ been purpofely left with a blank page (either worked-off
‘ or not), until the blank page could be filled up with a
‘ Preface, in which the Editors, conformably to rea-
‘ fon, might fpeak of their performance as of a work
‘ already executed.—*Secondly,* That, without going a great
‘ way for an actual example of what I fuppofe *may* have
‘ been practifed in this cafe, a fhining example of it we
‘ have at hand in the very next ninth and laft volume,
‘ the final date of which fpecifying the month of *May*
‘ 1516,

peregrinationis causa, to whom he eagerly applied:
and that, from his intercourse with them he had
acquired

' 1516, the Preface neverthelefs is dated *June* the 26
' *(Sexto Kalendas Julias).*—*Thirdly*, That, of all the dates
' in the whole fet which mark the month, the oldeft being
' (T. II. fol. verfo 191) of Auguft 1515, none is fo late in
' 1516 as that of the Polyglott Pfalter in queftion. From
' which reafons it is plain to me that the book might have
' been ready for fale, if not precifely on the 25th of Auguft
' (VIII *Calend. Septembreis)* at fartheft a few days after;
' two months, not to fay three, before Porrus had printed
' his final date of *November*, without marking the day;
' which, if one of the laft in the month, he had fome rea-
' fon to fuppref, that it might not look near four full
' months remote from the firft of Auguft; this being the
' date of Juftiniani's dedication to the Pope, and the dedi-
' cation having probably been printed when he hoped, and
' perhaps promifed, that againft fuch a time the whole
' fhould be finifhed. But, be this as it will, I think I have
' faid enough to make good what I hinted above, that the
' Polyglott Pfalter of Bafil might difpute the precedency
' with that of Genoa.——By all this, however, I am far
' from pretending to make *Erafmus* the firft Editor of
' Polyglott Books: and I firmly believe that when Le
' Long inferted thefe words, *Cura & ftudio Defid. Erafmi*,
' he did it without any other foundation than the common
' opinion which afcribes to *Erafmus* the whole bufinef of
' preparing this Edition of Jerom's works; though he fo
' little meddled with Hebrew, that when he had occafion
' for it, *en paffant*, he would not proceed without requiring
' the affiftance of the two brothers *Bruno* and *Bafil Amer-*
                                                    ' *bach.*

acquired fuch a knowledge of their language, as to
make him believe he might undertake an edition of
the

‘ bach. So that Le Long, inftead of *Cura & ftudio Defid.*
‘ *Erafmi*, might rather have faid, *Cura & ftudio Brunonis*
‘ *& Bafilii Amerbachiorum* (or, as they ufed to fpell it,
‘ *Amorbachiorum*). This I infer from their joint Addrefs
‘ to the Reader, at the head of Tome the Fifth ; where
‘ alfo the Reader is informed of fome particulars which
‘ may ferve as a good, or even neceffary, comment upon
‘ the fifth page of Erafmus's dedication to Archbifhop
‘ Warham. I. That when Erafmus [who by the bye had
‘ himfelf collected materials towards an edition by him in-
‘ tended of St. Jerom's works] came to Bafil ; he found
‘ great provifions and preparations already made [for the
‘ fame purpofe] ; at the expence, and by the care, of their
‘ now deceafed Father, *John Amerbach :* who, after pro-
‘ curing St. Ambrofe's and St. Auftin's works, printed
‘ *fuis typis*, had refolved to go on with St. Jerom's. II. That
‘ their father, intending to make them collaborators in
‘ that work, had furnifhed them with fome knowledge
‘ (*qualicunque peritia*, as they term it) in the Latin, Greek,
‘ and Hebrew languages. III. That Erafmus having taken
‘ upon him the care of the four firft Tomes, the care of
‘ the five laft became their lot. And accordingly, in all
‘ the fubfequent Addreffes to the Reader, we find them
‘ (though under the fole name of *Bruno)* fpeaking as
‘ Editors ; yet making honourable mention of the Learned
‘ to whofe affiftance they acknowledged themfelves much
‘ indebted. And let me add, that they not only never fpeak
‘ as Printers, but exprefs themfelves in fuch a manner as
‘ to leave all the honours of the printing-office to *John*
‘ *Froben :*

the Æthiopic Pfalter; which was actually publifhed at Rome nearly five years before the date of his Polyglott performance. At the end of the above-

' *Froben:* fo that, in Le Long's account, it was a new
' miftake to write *Typis Amerbachii:* a miftake, however,
' which Maittaire himfelf, in *his* account, has not avoided,
' his words being, p. 124: *Eodem anno quo Juftinianus fuum*
' *Pfalterium Pentaglotton edidit;* *Bafileæ ab Amorbachio Pfalte-*
' *rium triglotton . . . excufum eft.*—Something more might be
' added in order to rectify by the prefent account of Eraf-
' mus's Jerom, fome inaccuracies which may puzzle or
' miflead the reader, in the accounts given of it by the
' very beft and lateft writers of Erafmus's Life: but I
' think that this hint alone may be fufficient. The only
' addition in which I fhall indulge myfelf, will be to prefent
' the Reader with a kind of Infcription in capitals, which is
' very confpicuous at the end of the laft volume; and by
' which we may be made, in fome meafure, to underftand,
' not only how far Froben is to be looked upon as connected
' with, or diftinguifhed from, the Amerbachs; but alfo, what
' that *Society* was, which I remember is fomewhere fpoken of
' by Erafmus himfelf, (if I miftake not) who relates, that on
' his refufing with fom obftinacy a confiderable fum offered
' him by Froben, and urging that he thought fuch a fum
' too confiderable from a man even in his circumftances,
' Froben at laft prevailed by affuring him, that the offer he
' made was not at his own private expence, but at the ex-
' pence of the *Society*. The faid Infcription is as follows:
" BASILEAE IN AEDIBVS IO. FROBENNII IMPENDIO
" BRVNONIS, BASILII ET BONIFACII AMORBACHIORVM,
" AC IOANNIS FROBENNII CHALCOGRAPHI ET IACOBI
" RECHBVRGII CIVIVM BASILIENSIVM. MENSE MAIO.
" AN. M.D.XVI."

S   mentioned

mentioned addrefs, he promifed to perform fomething in the Arabic, if he fhould meet with fufficient
encouragement.

The famous Bible of Cardinal XIMENES, com-
monly called the *Complutenfian*, confifts of fix large folio
volumes; having the Hebrew [d], Latin, and Greek
in three diftinct columns, and the Chaldee paraphrafe,
with a Latin interpretation, at the bottom of the
page, the margin being filled with the Hebrew and
Chaldee radicals. It was begun in 1502, finifhed
in 1517, but not publifhed till 1522. A more particular account of it may be feen in LE LONG, and
in MAITTAIRE [e].

In 1546 appeared, at Conftantinople, " Penta-
" teuchus Hebræo-Chaldæo-Perfico-Arabicus," in
three columns; the Hebrew text in the middle; on
the right hand the Perfic verfion of R. JACOB fil.
JOSEPH; and on the left the Chaldee paraphrafe of

[d] The Hebrew text in this edition was corrected by
ALPHONSUS, a phyfician of Complutum, PAULUS CORO-
NELLUS, and ALPHONSUS ZAMORA, who were all con-
verts from Judaifm to Chriftianity. The Mff. it was printed
from had undergone the Maforetical caftigation. See Dr.
KENNICOTT, Diff. II. p. 475.

[e] The Gentleman to whom we are indebted for the
obfervations on POTKEN's *Pfalter* would have favoured us
with fome curious remarks on this fcarce edition, and on
that of Antwerp by PLANTINUS, but had not leifure to get
them ready in time. We hope, however, to be able
fpeedily to prefent them to the Public, as a Supplement to
the prefent publication.

ONKELOS:

ONKELOS: at the top is the Arabic paraphrafe of
SAADIAS, and at the bottom the commentary of RASI.
The whole is printed in Hebrew characters with
points, the middle column on a larger fize than the
others. At the end of Genefis appears, " Abfolutus
" eft liber Genefeos in domo ELIEZERIS BERAB
" GERSON Soncinatis [f]."

In 1547, was publifhed, from the fame prefs, " Pen-
" tateuchus Hebraicus, Hifpanicus, & Barbaro-Græ-
" cus." This edition was alfo printed in three columns; the Hebrew Text in the middle; the old
Spanifh verfion on the right hand; and on the left,
the *modern* Greek, as ufed by the Caraïtes at Conftantinople, who do not underftand Hebrew. The
Spanifh is defigned for the Refugee Spanifh Jews.
At the head and bottom of the pages are the Targum and the Commentary as in the laft mentioned
editions [g].

The next Polyglott Bible (commonly called the
Royal or *Spanifh* Polyglott) was printed at Antwerp,
by CHRISTOPHER PLANTINUS 1569—1572, by au-
thority of Philip II, King of Spain, in Hebrew,
Greek, Latin, and Chaldee, under the direction of
ARIAS MONTANUS, in eight volumes, folio. The
New Teftament had alfo the Syriac verfion [h].

In

[f] LE LONG, p. 45.   [g] Ibid. p. 46.
[h] " We need fay the lefs of this great work ; as it is
" not pretended, that the leaft *correction* was made in this
" edition of the Hebrew Text. Indeed no fuch thing could
" poffibly be expected from an Editor who believed the

S 2   " per-

In 1586 a Polyglott Bible was publifhed at Heidelberg, in two volumes, folio; printed in four columns, Hebrew, Greek, and two Latin verfions, viz. St. Jerom's and that of *Santes Pagninus*; with the notes of VATABLUS; and in the margin are the idioms, and the *radices* of all the difficult words.   Two other dates have been feen to this edition, viz. 1599 and 1616; but LE LONG, after an attentive comparifon, declares them to be only different copies of the fame impreffion; but that fome of them have the Greek Teftament with the addition of the Latin verfion of ARIAS MONTANUS [*i*].

In 1596, JACOBUS LUCIUS printed an edition, in Greek, Latin, and German, at Hamburgh, in four volumes, folio, "Studio DAVIDIS WOLDERI," the Greek from the Venice edition of 1518 [*k*]; the Latin verfions of St. JEROM and PAGNINUS.

In

"perfection of the Hebrew Text—*quanta integritate* (fays
"he) *femper confervata fuerint Biblia Hebræa, plerique doc-*
"*tiffimi viri conflanter affeverarunt,* &c. HODY, p. 516,
"517." Dr. KENNICOTT, Diff. II. p. 477.   This edition
is particularly defcribed in LE LONG, p. 20.

[*i*] "Quæ fub VATABLI nomine circumferuntur Biblia,
"ejus non funt; annotationefque eidem adfcriptæ auctorem
"habent ROBERTUM STEPHANUM." WALTON, Proleg.
iv. p. 33.   See LONG, p. 15.

[*k*] LE LONG, p. 26.—FABRICIUS, *Bibliotheca Græca*,
fays the fame.   But the editor, WOLDERUS himfelf, in his
Preface fpeaks thus : "De LXX interpretum Grecâ, deque
"Latinâ HIERONYMI, ut putatur, verfione nihil moneo :
nifi

In 1599 ELIAS HUTTERUS publifhed one at No-
remberg, in fix languages; four of them, the Hebrew,
Chaldee, Greek, and Latin, printed from the Antwerp edition; the fifth was the German verfion of
LUTHER; and the fixth the Sclavonic verfion of Wit-
temberg [*l*]. This Bible was never completed, but
goes no farther than the book of *Ruth*.

In

" nifi quod fcire tua non parum, opinor, intereft; in iis,
" Plantiniaram editionem me effe fequutum : quod cor-
" rectior quidem quæ effet nulla fefe mihi offerret." As
far as can be judged from a collation of fome paffages, it
appears that he followed the edition of PLANTINUS, but
ufed his own judgement in the punctuation, and other lefs
material particulars. The new Latin verfion, here printed,
appears to be, not that of PAGNINUS (though faid to be
his by WOLDERUS); but rather that which ROBERT STE-
PHENS publifhed in 1557, corrected from the obfervations of
PAGNINUS and VATABLUS. The New Teftament is the
firft of BEZA, which R. STEPHENS printed in 1556, with
the fame types which he ufed in the following year for the
abovementioned Latin verfion of the Old Teftament.—
We are indebted for this note to the Mf. annotations which
the Rev. Mr. DE MISSY had made many years ago on the
margin of his copy of LE LONG's *Bibliotheca Sacra*, fuch
as it is in the Leipfic edition of 1709.

[*l*] Inftead of the Sclavonic, fome copies were printed
with the French verfion of Geneva; others, with the Italian of the fame city; and others again with a Saxon verfion from the German of LUTHER.—HUTTERUS publifhed
the Pfalter and New Teftament in Hebrew, Greek, Latin,
and German. He alfo publifhed the New Teftament in

5   TWELVE

In 1645 was printed, by ANTHONY VITRE, Monf.
LE JAY's Polyglott Bible, in Hebrew, Samaritan,
Chaldee, Greek, Syriac, Arabic, and Latin; in the
title faid to be, " *Parifiis*, MDCXXVI et ann. feqq. ad
" MDCXLV," in ten volumes [*m*].

Dr. BRIAN WALTON publifhed the London Polyglott in NINE languages, Hebrew, Samaritan, Chaldee, Greek, Syriac, Arabic, Ethiopic, Perfic, and Latin, in 1657 [*n*]. This edition has been fuppofed by
Mr.

TWELVE languages; viz. Syriac, Hebrew, Greek, Italian,
Spanifh, and French, in one page; and Latin, German,
Bohemian, Englifh, Danifh, and Polonefe, in another.
CALMET, ubi fupra. See LE LONG, p. 26.

[*m*] LE LONG, p. 27. PALMER, p. 274. This edition
is remarkable for the Samaritan Pentateuch having been
firft printed in it, with its verfion, from Mff. brought into
Europe between the year 1620 and 1630, under the care of
the very learned MORINUS. See Dr. KENNICOTT, Diff. II.
p. 478.

[*n*] Though *nine* languages are ufed in this edition, there
is no *one* book in the whole Bible printed in fo many. In
the New Teftament the Four Evangelifts are in *fix* languages, the other books only in five. The books of Judith
and the Maccabees are only in *three* languages. The Septuagint verfion is printed from the edition at Rome Anno 1587.
The Latin is the Vulgate of CLEMENT VIII. The Chaldee
Paraphrafe is completer than any former publication. This
edition is enriched with Prefaces, Prolegomena, Treatifes on
Weights and Meafures, Geographical Charts, and Chrono-
logical Tables. CALMET, ubi fupra, p. viii.—Dr. WAL-
TON was affifted in this laborious undertaking by Dr.
EDMUND

Mr. PALMER to have been printed from sheets surreptitiously obtained from the press at Paris; and to have been published with improvements so soon after, as to reduce M. LE JAY almost to want, after having expended above £. 5000 sterling to compleat his work. But Mr. PALMER mistook the date of LE JAY's *Polyglott* (which he makes to be 1657), and

EDMUND CASTELL, who translated from the Syriac some fragments of Daniel, the books of Tobit and Judith, the Letters of Jeremiah and Baruch, and the first book of the Maccabees; he also translated the Song of Solomon from the Æthiopic into Latin, and added notes to the Samaritan Pentateuch; but the most considerable assistance he gave was by his Lexicon in two volumes, a work which is a necessary supplement to the Polyglott. ALEXANDER HUISSE *collected* the *various Readings* at the bottom of each page; revised the Septuagint version, the Greek Text of the New Testament, and the Latin Vulgate; he also collated the edition of the Old Testament printed at Rome, and the New Testament of ROBERT STEPHENS, with the Alexandrine manuscript. See PRIDEAUX, vol. II. p. 47. Dr. THOMAS HYDE corrected the Arabic, Syriac, and Persic; as LOFTUSIUS did the Æthiopic version of the New Testament. LOUIS LE DIEU and SAMUEL CLARKE were also assistants in the work. LE LONG, p. 33, &c.—"The immense " merit of this work is too well known to need any la-" boured recommendation. And yet, it must be observed, " that in *This*, the best and most useful of all editions, the " Hebrew Text is printed *Maforetically*; almost in an ab-" solute agreement with the many former editions, and with " the latest and worst MSS." KENNICOTT, Diss. II. p. 480.

then

then formed his conclufion of the fheets being fent into England from Paris; and met with a correfpondent, it feems, that encouraged his error. LE JAY's *Polyglott* was publifhed, in Ten Volumes, MDCXLV : The Englifh *Polyglott*, in Six Volumes, not till MDCLVII, twelve years after the other [*o*] ; under Dr. WALTON's picture, we are told it was begun only in MDCLIII.—It is faid indeed that the Englifh put out *Propofals* for a cheaper and better edition, foon after LE JAY's was publifhed, which might in fome meafure hinder the fale of it. But other caufes concurred. The enormous fize of the book rendered it inconvenient for ufe ; and the price deterred purchafers. And further, the refufal of LE JAY to publifh it under RICHELIEU's name, though that Minifter had offered to print it at his own expence,

[*o*] Dr. WALTON got leave to import paper, duty-free, in 1652 ; began the work 1653; and publifhed it 1657. It is furprizing he could get through fix fuch volumes in four years ; though certainly many Printers were employed on it; among others, Mr. ICHABOD DAWES of Lowlayton, maternal grandfather to W. BOWYER. But it is plain that, in the re-printed leaf of the Preface, Dr. WALTON robs the Protector of the honour of patronizing this work, which was begun in 1653, and publifhed in 1657 ; three years before the Reftoration, 1660. The licence was granted by the Council of State in 1652; and was continued by OLIVER, who diffolved the Rump-Parliament in 1653. Dr. WALTON was confecrated Bifhop of CHESTER December 2, 1660; and died Nov. 29, 1661.

damped

damped the fale of it.—The Englifh Polyglott, in
return, made but little way in France. A large-paper
copy was fold, in 1718, to a gentleman of the name
of COLBERT, the fix volumes bound in fourteen.
CASTELL's *Lexicon*, that went along with this fet,
was on a fmaller-fized paper: The fame copy was
afterwards fold to M. DE SEUL, and is now in the
collection of the Count DE LAURAGUAIS [*p*].

The laft leaf but one of the Preface of WALTON's
Polyglott is canceled in many copies; a circumftan-
tial account of which we are enabled to lay before
the Reader in the words of a Friend, to whom this
Appendix is already moft materially indebted.

" To Mr. BOWYER.

" DEAR SIR,

" I will venture to be pofitive, that I never fpoke
" a word before this, concerning two different *Dedi-*
" *cations* of WALTON's Polyglott; though I remem-
" ber fomething that may have been the occafion of
" fomebody's thinking I did. The fact is, to the beft.
" of my remembrance,

" I. That when we met at Cambridge [nineteen or
" twenty years ago], and, in company with feveral
" other perfons, vifited the Library of Trinity-Col-

[*p*] DE BURE, Bibliographie Inftructive des Belles Letres,
vol. I. p. 18.

T   " lege,

" lege, a gentleman, on my taking notice there were
" two copies of the faid Polyglott, dropt a hint
" about exchanging duplicates for other books:

" II. That upon this I made bold to obferve—Du-
" plicates were not always a mere fuperfluity, efpe-
" cially in public libraries, where they might have
" been intended to be kept together for curiofity's
" fake, on account of fome remarkable difference be-
" tween them; which might even be the cafe with
" the very books juft taken notice of:

" III. That accordingly, the firft volume of one
" copy being compared with the firft volume of the
" other, one of the two was found to have in the
" *Preface* what its companion had not, a compliment
" for (or acknowledgment of obligation to) *the Lord*
" *Protector and his Council*; which I think is only
" preferved in the few copies that were difpofed of
" before the Reftoration, and perhaps not in all of
" them; fince the fame courtly loyalty by which the
" Republican leaf containing the faid compliment had
" been canceled, might very well induce fome prudent
" or cunning people to tear it out of the copies in
" their poffeffion, and get it replaced by its more
" loyal fubftitute, the reprinted leaf; in which Crom-
" well's praife is not more to be looked for, than his
" bones in the Chapel of Henry the Seventh:

" IV. That in the firft edition of the faid leaf,
" where the compliment for *the Protector and his*
" *Council* offers itfelf connected with a previous com-
" pliment of the fame kind for *another Council ante-*

2   " *cedent*

" cedent to Cromwell's Protectorate, we found this (the
" laft mentioned compliment) fo introduced and fo
" worded, as Walton's profeffed gratitude naturally
" would have it to be : inftead of which, the fecond
" edition has nothing but a faint fhadow of it, in a
" few vague words, introduced only by way of pa-
" renthefis ; and fo well chofen, however, that un-
" cautious readers might as eafily take them for an
" indifpenfable act of gratitude to the King's Council,
" as for a joyful effufion of gratitude to a Council,
" fet up by his enemies : the different readings of the
" two editions (both with regard to Cromwell or his
" Council, and the Privy-Council of the Common-
" wealth) being exactly fuch as you fhall fee prefently ;
" unlefs I made fome blunder in tranfcribing, from
" the firft edition, the moft material part of the
" paffage they belong to ; which indeed was dif-
" patched in a great hurry, while the company near
" me were talking (ut fit) about any thing elfe.

" Suppofing then a full agreement of the two edi-
" tions as far as I took notice of no variety, the whole
" paffage in the firft muft be deemed to run as follows :
" fave only that I fhall write in large capitals the word
" which makes the beginning of the place that has
" been altered : " Utque eorum conatus qui collatis
" ftudiis adjumento nobis fuerunt lubenter agnofci-
" mus, fic nullo non obfequii genere profequendi
" Mæcenates munifici, qui ubertim donaria fua ad
" facrum opus promovendum obtulerunt, quorum
" meritis cum pares non fimus, quod unum poffu-

T 2   " mus,

" mus, grata mente recolimus, & in devotiſſimæ
" obſervantiæ, perpetuique cultus & obſequii ſignum,
" beneficentiam eorum hic omnibus teſtatam facimus.
" PRIMO autem commemorandi, quorum favore
" chartam à vectigalibus immunem habuimus, quod
" quinque abhinc annis, a *Concilio* ſecretiori, primo
" conceſſum, poſtea à Sereniſſimo D Protectore
" ejuſque *Concilio*, operis promovendi caúſa, benigne
" confirmatum &. continuatum erat. Quibus ſub-
" jungendi, D. Carolus Ludovicus, princeps Pala-
" tin. S. R. I. Elector : Illuſtriſſimus D. Gulielmus
" &c." In my copy, which is one of the loyal ſort,
" the latter part lof the paſſage (from the word
" PRIMO, down to the name *Carolus*) is reformed or
" transformed. in this manner : " Inter hos effuſiore
" bonitate labores noſtros proſecuti ſunt (praeter eos
" quorum favore chartam à vectigalibus immunem ha-
" buimus) Sereniſſimus Princeps D. Carolus &c."

" All I can ſay further on this ſubject is, that the
" paſſage I ſpeak of being the only one I collated,
" ſomething more perhaps of the ſame kind might
" be diſcovered by a more extenſive collation. The
" page that contains the paſſage is the laſt-but-one
" of the Preface, and the *ſecond* of the reprinted
" leaf; in the *firſt* of which (at a ſmall diſtance
" from the-bottom) I obſerve that Walton, mention-
" ing what we may call his *literary* obligations to
" ſome eminent churchmen, once chaplains to the
" unfortunate Charles, not only ſtiles them *Sacræ*
" *Theo-*

" *Theologiæ Doctores*, but addeth, *& Regi Carolo τῷ*
" ἐν ἁγίοις *olim Capellani* [*q*]. Now this place at leaſt
" (I own) I ſhould like to compare with the firſt im-
" preſſion, and I am ſorry I took no notice of it
" when I had an opportunity; though indeed not ſo
" ſorry on that account, as on account of having
" made you ſtay ſo long for an anſwer; which how-
" ever would have been ready much ſooner, had my
" health better agreed with my inclination to ſhew
" myſelf,

" Dear Sir,

" Your moſt obedient

Balſover-Street,
21 April, 1770,

" humble ſervant,

" CÆSAR DE-MISSY."

[*q*] The following variations have been noticed in the
leaf of the *Preface* which immediately precedes this, and
which appears alſo to have been re-printed :

P. 7. *l. ult:* impoſuimus *(as it ſtood in what may be called the*
Republican *copy) is changed into* appoſuimus
P. 8. *l.* 7. exhibeatur *into* exhibetur
l. 27. impulcrint ut opus *into* impulerint ut temporibus
hiſce turbulentis, cum Religio et literæ Oſtracif-
mum quaſi paſſæ videantur, opus, B.

Before

Before we quit this edition, we shall take the liberty to observe, on the authority, and in the words,
of the critical Friend to whom we are indebted for
the Hebrew collation in our Appendix N° II, that
" the latter part of the English Polyglott is much
" more incorrectly printed than the former; pro-
" bably either owing to the Editor's absence from
" the press, or to his being over-fatigued by the
" work. This will appear in very obvious instances,
" if we cast our eye only on the title *Targum Jona-*
" *than* תרגום יונתן. which is often printed falsely
" in Hosea, Joel, Amos, Micah, Nahum, Zechariah,
" particularly ch. xiv. p. 138, where both words are
" misprinted.

" But this is not the worst. The *Hebrew Text* suf-
" fered much in several places by the rapidity of the
" publication. To multiply instances would be invi-
" dious. I shall therefore mention only one; which
" occurs in Gen. xxxiv. 1. where we read דינא in-
" stead of דינה.

" There is also in the *Samaritan* Text, according
" to the *English* Polyglott, a very grievous blunder;
" entirely owing to the heedless transposition of two
" words ערב and, בקר, Gen. i. 19, by which that
" text, in contradiction to itself elsewhere, says, " and
" the *morning* and the *evening* were the fourth day."
" And this, as the *translation* is different, I take
" to have been an error of the Editor, and not of
" the copy from which he printed.

" Nor

" Nor is this the only error, for in Gen. iii. 2. הכחש
" is falfely printed for הנחש. So again Gen. iv. 5.
" מנחתו for מנחמו.

" But this is nothing, comparatively fpeaking, to
" what we meet with a little below, at ver. 7. where
" the fecond תטיב is unluckily omitted in its proper
" place; and then inferted after רבץ, with a repeti-
" tion of the word לפתח, to the utter confufion of
" the fenfe of the paffage—for literally tranflated it
" runs thus: *Nonne, fi benefeceris, recipies? fi autem*
" *non, ad portam peccatum cubat, benefeceris ad portam.*

" Thefe are glaring inftances of unpardonable ne-
" gligence; and the more unpardonable, becaufe they
" ftand at the *entrance* of a work, which juftly re-
" quired the greateft care, and the utmoft accu-
" racy.

" I fhall only add, what, in obedience to truth, I
" am bound to add, that the *French* Polyglott is en-
" tirely clear of all *thefe* errors; and indeed of many
" *others*, which the attentive Reader will find fcat-
" tered through the *Englifh* Polyglott."

In the *Preface* alfo are the following inaccuracies:

P. 1. *laft paragraph but one*, r, κοἰακλυσμὸς *
3. *l*. 1. *for* variant *r*. varient

* WALTON's word is κατακλύσματα, which makes an odd appearance at the head of fuch *inaccuracies* as are mere *Errata Typographica*.
The word was probably of his own making; and he might take it
to be formed as regularly as ἐκκλύσματα. C. D. M.

P. 3.

P. 3. *l.* 23 *for* 1615 *r.* 1515

 l. 15 *from bottom, for* Teſtmenti *r.* Teſtamenti

P. 5. *l.* 23 *for* Quinti *r.* Quarti

 l. 22 *from bottom, for* Pariſ. ex *r.* Pariſ. quæ ex

 l. 5 *from bottom, for* opus in *r.* opus ni

P. 6. *l.* 20 *for* occurrunt *r.* occurrit †

 l. 17 *from bottom, for* Plantina *r.* Plantini ‡

 l. 7 *from bottom, for* Haphtorarum *r.* Haphtararum

P. 9. *l.* 20 *from bottom, for* pertimeſeret *r.* pertimeſceret.

† The place is certainly faulty, as *quicquid* . . . . *occurrunt* will never paſs. But in what word the fault lies is perhaps not ſo certain. Perhaps, for *quicquid,* we ſhould read *quæcunque.* C. D. M.

‡ This whole line is very bad, and a thorough reviſion of it would, perhaps, make us queſtion whether *Plantiniana* for *Plantina* would not do as well as *Plantini.* C. D. M.

[143]

ADDENDUM to Note [Z], p. 92.

" Having not Mr. Köhlerus's book, I can but guefs how
" *Deborah* comes in there with *Chriſtina*; and the only
" thing I can guefs is, that Köhlerus, in order to evince the
" poſſibility of *Dynen* being a diminutive of *Chriſtina*, had
" alledged, as an example of a ſtill ſhorter diminutive, the
" uſe of *Deb* for *Deborah :* which, if he did, Mr. Meerman's
" ſeeming to wonder at it may be tolerably accounted for.
" But what, if inſtead of theſe diminutives that retain only
" the beginning of a name, he had mentioned ſome of thoſe
" which retain only the latter part of it, and that not al-
" ways entire, as our *Bell* for *Arabella*, *Mun* for *Edmund*,
" *Tony* for *Antony*, *Sander* for *Alexander*, *Bet* or *Betty* for
" *Elizabeth* ? Mr. Meerman's own book furniſhes us (vol. II,
" p. 79) with a liſt of German names, among which,
" *Hans* clearly appears for *Johans* or *Johannes*, *Claus* for
" *Nicolaus*, and, if I miſtake not, *Neſe* for *Agnes*. Such
" examples make it certainly plauſible enough that *Tynen*,
" or the ſame lovingly ſoftened into *Dynen*, might be a di-
" minutive of *Chriſtynen*, which (or elſe *Chriſtynin*) I take
" to be the feminine for *Chriſtyn*, as *Fuſtin*, or *Fuſten*, is
" the feminine for *Fuſt*. See vol. I. p. 184. where this
" very daughter of *Fuſt*, is called *Fuſtbin*, but where *th*
" imports no more than *t*. And ſuppoſing now that all this
" ſhould be deemed inſufficient to ſolve the queſtion how
" John Schoeffer could call his mother *Chriſtina*, while it
" appears that his father, in a convention paſſed between
" himſelf and his kinſman, *John Fuſt*, ſon of *John*, has
" called her by the name of *Dynen*; there is, I think, an-
" other ſolution ready, in the obvious ſuppoſition that ſhe
" might have two names, and that he, eſpecially in a writing
" paſſed with a kinſman, might have choſen, as a loving
" huſband, to call her familiarly by what I muſt be al-
" lowed to term the favourite name." C. D. M.

U ADDEN-

ADDENDUM to Note [U], p. 90.

" Mr. MEERMAN's explanation is intricate at leaſt ; and
" it leaves us beſides to wonder, not ónly how *forms of*
" *letters* could be bare bodies or pieces of metal *without*
" *letters,* but how ſo conſiderable a part of the invention as
" the matrices ſhould have been only mentioned indirectly
" as a thing well known before. A correction, however,
" ſeems abſolutely neceſſary. Neither can it be denied that
" Mr. MEERMAN, by inſerting *ex eis,* clears TRITHEMIUS
" from the reproach of ſaying, that even matrices were
" made by way of *fuſion* ; and thus far I like his correction
" ſo well, that I am ſorry to ſee the new difficulties ariſing
" from it in the context, notwithſtanding his elaboráte ex-
" planation ; which, had I room and leiſure to make it
" plainer by a compleat paraphraſe, I ſhould rather leave
" as it is ; becauſe all the machines required for ſuch a
" paraphraſe, would only ſerve to ſet in a clearer light the
" intricacy of the affair, while ſomething better perhaps may
" be done to obtain what ſeems to have been Mr. MEERMAN's
" chief end. Something certainly is faulty in TRITHE-
" MIUS's phraſe, *fundendi formas .. quas ipſi matrices nomi-*
" *nabant.* But then, why ſhould not the fault be ſuſpected
" to lie in that very unlucky word which properly conſti-
" tutes the acknowledged abſurdity of the phraſe ? I think,
" in ſhort, that by ſome ſpot or accidental ſtroke of
" the pen in the Mſ. the word *cudendi* might have been
" miſtaken for *fūdendi :* nay, I think, that even the more
" ſimilar word *tundendi* might have been employed by
" TRITHEMIUS, as being not altogether improper, ſince
" it could be interpreted, at leaſt with the help of ſome in-
" dulgence, by *Tudite vel tudicula imprimendi* ; not to ſay
" that, according to the well-known obſervation, *Verbum*
" *ſimplex ſaepe ponitur pro compoſito,* the ſimple word *tundendi*
" might be taken in a ſenſe analagous to the compound
" *pertundendi.* I can ſay no more at preſent." C. D. M.